What people are saying about *Christian Faith and Same-Sex Attraction*:

"This book reflects the deep wisdom of the Orthodox Christian tradition on one of the most urgent and controversial issues of our day. The argument is closely reasoned and touches on many aspects of this issue that are often ignored in popular presentations. This is not a new issue, and Father Hopko draws on the accumulated wisdom of the saints and sages of the Great Tradition, not to say the Holy Scriptures, in helping us to understand same-sex attraction in a world that is at once fallen and being redeemed by the God of grace and glory. A provocative book that will surely help everyone who reads it!"
   —*Timothy George, Dean of Beeson Divinity School of Samford University; an executive editor of* Christianity Today

"With moral wisdom and pastoral attentiveness to the wounded and perplexed, Father Hopko addresses questions much disputed in our culture and in Christian communities. In a winsomely accessible manner, he draws on the treasures of Orthodoxy to invite all of us to move from disputation to reflection, and from there to the wholeness for which we are created by God."
   —*Richard John Neuhaus, Editor-in-Chief of* First Things

"Although I profoundly disagree with the stance taken towards homosexuality in this book I found it a delight to read. It is a careful, compassionate and comprehensive discussion of contemporary same-sex attraction from the perspective of the Orthodox tradition. It is informed by gay and lesbian theology and other alternative perspectives. I would recommend it to all who study or who are personally involved in the issues around same-sex relationships in the Christian tradition, perhaps particularly to those not part of the Orthodox tradition, for the rich theology of that tradition frames the debate in very different terms to those of other denominations. This book holds out the possibility of a debate which need not fracture the Church nor create alarming levels of animosity between Christians. For this reason alone, it is worth reading and engaging with."
   —*Elizabeth Stuart, Professor of Christian Theology , The University of Winchester; Author of* Gay & Lesbian Theologies: Repetitions With Critical Difference.

"Fr. Hopko explains why 'gay' can never be 'who a person is' in the deepest sense. Human nature was created good. Sexual union is meant to be complementary, unitive, life-creating, and life-enhancing. The corruption of this fallen world, however, causes us to misdirect our sexual energies into channels the Creator never intended. Same-sex eroticism is one of many expressions of our deformed humanity.

"This book is full of sage advice to Christians struggling with homosexuality, advising men and women to seek wise counsel from a same-sex mentor, and—against almost all the advice of today's popular culture—inspiring them to a holy asceticism for the sake of virtue."

—*Joseph Nicolosi, Ph.D.*, *President, NARTH, Exodus International Speakers Bureau*

"This thoughtful and comprehensive little volume is valuable for all Christians. Stating the issue in terms of 'same-sex attraction' and 'sexual feelings and predispositions' is immensely helpful in an age immersed in unclear and confusing language. I particularly find Father Hopko's treatment of ancestral and generational sins significant. I warmly recommend this excellent and insightful book."

—*Dr. John H. Armstrong*, *President, Act 3, Carol Stream, Illinois*

"Already in the mid-1980s, Fr. Hopko identified human sexuality as the most significant theological concern of our generation. Here he treats the difficult and delicate subject of same-sex attraction in an exceptionally well-balanced way. Both the text and the ample footnotes combine theological and pastoral insight to produce a virtual summa of Orthodox anthropology. The result is a work that offers clear and compassionate direction to those who experience same-sex attraction and to those who seek to minister to them. This study deserves the widest possible readership: by pastors and medical professionals, as well as by those who experience same-sex feelings and desires."

—*V. Rev. John Breck*, *Professor, St. Sergius Theological Institute, Paris, France*

"Father Hopko deftly handles the thorny questions about same-sex attraction. He has 20 years of experience in counseling those with homosexual tendencies and has written a book on how to overcome this particular passion with both grace and clarity. The result is a much-needed book which dispels the fog and provides guiding light. It helps us ponder our position, and provides a model for facing it candidly, while keeping our gaze on Jesus Christ. It is without reservation that I recommend this book to all."

—*Dr. Albert S. Rossi*, *Adjunct Professor at St. Vladimir's Seminary; Retired Professor, Pace University*

Christian Faith and SAME-SEX ATTRACTION

EASTERN

ORTHODOX

REFLECTIONS

BY THOMAS HOPKO

Conciliar Press
Ben Lomond, California

CHRISTIAN FAITH AND SAME-SEX ATTRACTION:
Eastern Orthodox Reflections
Copyright © 2006 Thomas Hopko

Published by   Conciliar Press
                P.O. Box 76
                Ben Lomond, California 95005-0076

ISBN 1-888212-75-6

Library of Congress Cataloging-in-Publication Data

Hopko, Thomas.
    Christian faith and same-sex attraction : Eastern Orthodox reflections /
    by Thomas Hopko.
        p. cm.
    Includes bibliographical references.
    ISBN 1-888212-75-6 (pbk.)
    1. Homosexuality–Religious aspects–Orthodox Eastern Church. I. Title.
BX323.H67 2006
261.8'35766082819–dc22

                                              2006042535

Contents

Author's Foreword

FRIENDS PERSUADED ME to abandon my efforts to write an introduction to this little book. They convinced me that the text must speak for itself not only about my convictions, but also about my intentions and hopes in agreeing to write it.

I thank my friends at Conciliar Press for asking me to do this work and for encouraging me to carry on when my heart fainted and my mind faltered. I also thank Fr. Michael Gillis for editing my convoluted writing, and for providing suggestions for improving the text. I especially thank my many friends who read many drafts and offered many criticisms and suggestions. They know who they are, and they surely know how grateful I am for their patience, truthfulness and love. I also thank many others who don't know me, or know me very little, whose words and writings on this subject are always with me.

These modest reflections are hardly exhaustive or final. I pray that they will be helpful, for God's glory and everyone's good.

Fr. Thomas Hopko
Elevation of the Cross
September 14, 2005

— 1 —

Christian Faith and Same-Sex Attraction

CHRISTIAN FAITH FOR EASTERN ORTHODOXY is a cluster of convictions about Jesus of Nazareth. The core conviction, in which all are rooted and around which all revolve, is that Jesus is "the Christ, the Son of the living God" foreknown and prefigured in the Law, Psalms, and prophetic writings of Israel (Matt. 16:16).[1]

Jesus, for Orthodoxy, is "the Lord's Christ."[2] He is also Himself "the Lord" together with God the Father and the Holy Spirit.[3] He is God's unique Son, Word, and Image in human flesh.[4] He is the Truth about God, humanity, and creation.[5] He is the Light and Life of the world, and of every person who comes into the world.[6] He is the eternal "Tao," the Way for all people to walk.[7]

Jesus "recapitulates" the story and Scriptures of Israel, the whole of human history, and all of creation in His divine and human Person.[8] He is "light from light, and true God from true God." He is begotten of God the Father before all ages and born as a human being from the Virgin Mary by the Holy Spirit.[9] He is before all things, and all things were made by Him and for Him, in whom they all hold together (Heb. 1:1–4; John 1:1–18). He is "the first-born over all creation" and "the firstborn from the dead," that He might be first in all things (Col. 1:15, 18). He is the divine Son of Man, the true and last Adam, "the man from heaven."[10] He is God's unique and final teacher, prophet, priest, pastor, king, and judge, whose messianic ministry is fulfilled in His death on the cross.[11] Having been crucified in shame, Jesus was raised from the dead by

God His Father, who "put all things under His feet," making "Him to be head over all things to the church, which is His body, the fullness of Him who fills all in all" (Eph. 1:19–23). [12]

Jesus reveals and fulfills everything about God, humanity, and creation in His death and resurrection. He deifies all things through His crucifixion and glorification. God's word for Orthodoxy is always "the word of the cross" (1 Cor. 1:18, RSV).[13] This word is foolishness to those seeking earthly wisdom and a scandal to those desiring earthly power. But for those who believe, the crucified Christ is God's wisdom and power. He is also God's righteousness, sanctification, and redemption (1 Cor. 1:22–31). In a word, the crucified Christ who is raised from the dead and enthroned at the right hand of the Father is, for Orthodox Christianity, everything for everyone. He is the victorious God and Lord who is "all and in all" *(Ta panta kai en pasin Christos!)*.[14]

1 NT writings insist that Jesus preached His messianic gospel, performed His messianic signs, and was crucified, raised, glorified, and proclaimed as Christ, Lord, and God "according to the scriptures [*kata tas graphas*]." See Luke 24:26–27, 32, 44–47; John 6:45–47; 12:16, 38–41; Acts 13:16–40; 17:2–3, 11; 18:28; 1 Cor. 15:3–4, and others.

2 Luke 2:26; Acts 2:22–36; Rom. 1:1–4; 2 Cor. 3:17, and others.

3 Mark 12:35–37; Matt. 22:41–45; Luke 21:41–44; John 20:28, and others.

4 Matt. 16:16; John 1:1–14; 3:16; 2 Cor. 4:4; Col. 1:15; Heb. 1:3, and others.

5 John 14:6; Eph. 4:20, and others.

6 John 8:12; 9:5; 11:9–10, 25; 12:46; 14:6; 1 John 1:1–7.

7 John 14:6; Acts 9:2. The biblical *Word* and the Hellenistic *Logos* find a counterpart in the Chinese *Tao*. See Hieromonk Damascene, *Christ the Eternal Tao* (Platina, CA: St. Herman's Brotherhood, 1999).

8 Recapitulation *(anakephalaiosis)* is a Pauline word and concept used by the church fathers, for example St. Irenaeus of Lyons. See Eph. 1; Col. 1:15 ff. Also Luke 24:26–27, 32, 44–47; 1 Cor. 15:3–6 ; 2 Cor. 3:12–16.

9 The Nicene-Constantinopolitan Creed. See John Behr, *The Way to Nicea* (Crestwood: SVS Press, 2001) and *The Nicene Faith* (Crestwood: SVS Press, 2004) for the scriptural foundations of Nicene Orthodoxy.

10 "Son of man" is a messianic title that Jesus applies to Himself in the Gospels. It evokes, among other things, the image in Daniel 7:9–14, joined with Psalm 110:1. Jesus repeatedly refers to the "Son of man coming on the clouds" in the apocalyptic passages of the synoptic Gospels, most significantly before the priests, scribes, and elders of the people at His Passion. Mark 12:35–37; 14:26, 62; Matt. 22:44; 24:30; 25:31; 26:63–64; Luke 21:27; 22:67–71. See also Rom. 5:14; 1 Cor. 15:42–50.

11 Jesus' final word on the cross according to St. John's Gospel, "*tetelestai* [it is finished]" (20:30), does not mean that His earthly life is ended. It rather means that in His act of dying, all acts of God on earth are accomplished, completed, and perfected. There is nothing more that God can reveal, say, show, or do. Everything is now fulfilled.

12 Ps. 110:1, quoted here, is perhaps the most cited OT verse in the NT writings: "The Lord said to my Lord, 'Sit at My right hand, till I make Your enemies Your footstool.'"

13 T. Hopko, *The Word of the Cross* [Audio CD] (Crestwood, NY: St. Vladimir's Seminary Press, 2005).

14 1 Cor. 15:26–28; Col. 3:11; John 20:28; and throughout Revelation.

— 2 —

Christt and the Church

THE "WHOLE CHRIST" FOR ORTHODOXY, however, is not Jesus alone.[1] The "whole Christ" is Jesus and His Church: Head and body, King and people, Pastor and flock, Master and disciples, Vine and branches, Cornerstone and temple. And of greatest importance for human sexuality, especially for the issue of same-sex love, the "whole Christ" is the divine and human Bridegroom together with His created, redeemed, and deified Bride.

The first title for Jesus in the Christian Gospels is "Bridegroom."[2] This is not surprising, since the prevalent image in the Bible for Yahweh's relation to Israel is that of conjugal love. God's kingdom is described as a marriage feast. It is the "marriage supper of the Lamb" (Rev. 19:7–9). The Church is the Lamb's "bride" and "wife" (Rev. 21:9). The "whole Christ"—already now for the Church, and forever for everyone in God's coming kingdom—is God's Son Jesus together with all men and women who by grace through faith become "one flesh" and "one spirit" with Him, thereby sharing in His Divine Sonship in the Holy Spirit.[3] The very bodies of believers who have the "mind of Christ" and the Spirit of God are, according to St. Paul, "members of Christ" (1 Cor. 2:16; 6:15).

According to Orthodox Christianity, Christians become one with God and grow forever in communion with Him through Christ and the Holy Spirit because they know how "wretched, miserable, poor, blind, and naked" they are (Rev. 3:17).[4] They acknowledge their desperate need for salvation and healing. They know that

11

without Jesus, they are lost and dead. They come to Christ, laboring and heavy laden, to learn from Him who is "gentle and lowly in heart." They find "rest for their souls" in Him whose "yoke is easy" and whose "burden is light" (Matt. 11:28–30).[5] They express their love for Him by keeping His commandments, which are not burdensome (John 14:15, 21; 1 John 5:3). They live with Him by dying with Him to this world and being raised with Him to "newness of life."[6] They abide in the constant remembrance and realization that they are not their own, but belong to Him who bought them by His blood to be His body and His Bride.[7]

1 The expression "whole Christ, head and body" is St. Augustine's well-known phrase: "*totus Christus, caput et corpus,*" *On St. John's Gospel,* 28:1, and others. See also St. Gregory of Nyssa, "in many places the Church is also called Christ by Paul," *Life of Moses,* 184; and "he who sees the Church looks directly at Christ. . . . The establishment of the Church is a re-creation of the world," *On the Song of Songs,* Sermon 13; also St. John Chrysostom, "For as the head and body are one man, so [the apostle Paul] said that the Church and Christ are one. Wherefore also he placed Christ instead of the Church, giving that name to His body," *On First Corinthians,* Homily 30.

2 Mark 2:19; John 3:29. The celebration of Christ's Passion in the Orthodox Church begins with the hymns "Behold, the Bridegroom comes" and "I see Your bridal chamber adorned." The liturgical services of the first days of Holy Week are called the Bridegroom Services. On Easter, the paschal canon proclaims that Christ comes forth from the tomb "like a Bridegroom in procession."

3 Eph. 5:23–32; 1 Cor. 6:15–19; and Gal. 3:23—4:7, which includes the baptismal processional hymn that replaces the Thrice-holy Hymn at the Divine Liturgy on great feasts in the Orthodox Church (3:27) and also the epistle reading at the Christmas liturgy (4:4–7). See also throughout Romans 8.

4 There is a story that St. Herman of Alaska asked some Russian sailors to come to church, and they responded that they could not do so because they were sinners. St. Herman replied that being a sinner was the sole qualification for being a Christian, and that only sinners are welcomed in church.

5 The word "easy," referring to Christ's yoke in the usual English translations, is "good" (*chrestos*) in the original Greek (*blago* in Slavonic). It is the word used in Ps. 34:8, "Oh, taste and see that the Lord is *good.*"

6 See Rom. 6:2–11, the epistle reading at the Vesperal Divine Liturgy of Pascha in the Orthodox Church and at Orthodox baptisms. See also Gal. 3:20; 6:14 and the hymn in 2 Tim. 2:11–13.

7 1 Cor. 6:20; 7:23; 2 Pet 2:1. The writings of St. Silouan of Mount Athos (d. 1938) are a simple, beautiful, and deceptively deep extended meditation on the points of this paragraph. They are found, with Archimandrite Sophrony Sakharov's long analytical introduction, in *Saint Silouan the Athonite* (Essex, England: Monastery of St. John the Baptist, 1999 and Crestwood, NY: SVS Press, 2000).

— 3 —

A Three-Dimensional Experience

THESE CONVICTIONS ABOUT CHRIST, and all things in Christ, with which we begin our reflections arise from an experience of reality that has three inseparable elements. If any of the three is lost, the experience, with the vision of reality it evokes, is destroyed. The first is that God made everything good as the created expression of His Divinity. The second is that everything has been corrupted and perverted by human sin. And the third is that everything is redeemed, sanctified, and glorified by the crucified and risen Christ.

Orthodox Christians receive this threefold experience, with the view of reality it produces, in the sacramental life of the Orthodox Church. They find it first witnessed in the Bible, every word of which, they believe, is ultimately about Christ crucified and glorified. They have it defined in the dogmatic definitions of the church councils. They have it explained in the writings of the church fathers. They have it protected by the Church's canons. They see it lived by the Church's saints, led by Christ's Mother Mary. They contemplate it in the icons. They celebrate it in the liturgy. They enter into it in the celebration of the Holy Eucharist by way of God's Word in the New Testament. And they strive to actualize it in their daily lives through ascetic struggle and ceaseless prayer.

The threefold experience—the goodness of creation, its corruption by creaturely evil, and its redemption and deification in Christ— illumines all things for those who repent, believe, and are baptized in the Orthodox Church.[1] This experience compels Orthodox believers to acknowledge that human beings are not "autonomous" in their humanity. It forces them to see that "another law" (*heteros nomos*)* is always working in their earthly members. This "other law" is either "the law of the Spirit of life in Christ Jesus" or "the law of sin and death" (Rom. 7:23; 8:2).[2] This threefold experience provides the criterion and frame of reference for all human experiences, and judges them all. It tests a person's subjective feelings, as well as the claims of science—especially the behavioral sciences, which study humanity in its sinful condition—as to their meaning and purpose for human being and life.

Our present task is to reflect on how this experience and vision of reality in Christ and the Church may apply to same-sex love and sexual activity, and so to love and sexual activity generally, as they are understood and enacted today, especially in North America, Europe, and Australia.

1 *Repent* means to change one's mind. *Believe* is to trust what one hears and sees. To be *baptized* is to die to one's former ideas and actions and to receive a new identity. Those who repent, believe, and are baptized in Christ receive His mind, act by His Spirit, and identify with Him in every way. See the first Christian sermon by the Apostle Peter on the day of Pentecost (Acts 2:14–42). Also Rom. 6:3–14, the epistle reading at the Vesperal Divine Liturgy of Pascha, and at baptisms in the Orthodox Church; Eph. 4:17–32; Col. 3:1–17.

2 See Rom. 7:21—8:30. The "law of the Spirit of life in Christ Jesus" (Rom. 8:2) is also simply called "the law of God" (Rom. 7:25). St. Paul also calls it "the law of Christ" (Gal. 6:2). The letter of James calls it "the perfect law of liberty" (James 1:25).

* Some Greek terms and phrases, usually having a technical meaning in traditional Christian writings, are provided in the text. Please ignore them if you find them distracting or unhelpful.

— 4 —

Same-Sex Attraction

I USE THE EXPRESSION "SAME-SEX ATTRACTION" in my reflections because I find the term "homosexuality," except in its most general usage, not very helpful.[1] It seems more accurate and useful to speak of persons with same-sex feelings and desires that have a wide variety of causes, forms, and expressions. I reflect on how these same-sex attractions and emotions relate to Christian faith as understood and experienced in Orthodox Christianity. And I especially try to reflect on how they relate to love, as revealed by God in Jesus Christ and the Holy Spirit in the Church.

According to Orthodox Christianity, all human persons are spiritual, psychic, and bodily beings created after the image and likeness of God.[2] They are made this way, male and female, to live forever in loving communion with God, each other, and the whole of creation.[3] Their calling and destiny is to become by God's grace all that God is by nature.[4]

For reasons that may never be completely or conclusively identified in any given person (though in some people they may be quite apparent), a small number of men and women have emotional feelings and erotic attractions, with desires for genital sexual activity, for persons of their own sex. Some claim to have had these feelings constantly and consistently their entire life, from earliest childhood. Others say that they have had them, and may continue to have them, only at certain times, or in certain situations, or under certain conditions.

In the Orthodox Christian view as I understand it, the phenomenon of same-sex attraction is originally due to humanity's rebellion against God. It is, in a word, an element in the second of the three dimensions of the Orthodox experience of reality to which we referred above: the corruption of the world by human sin. All our reflections here will return in different ways to this conviction, relating it to the other two fundamental convictions of Orthodoxy: namely, the foundational goodness of creation governed by men and women made in God's image and likeness; and God's salvation and deification of all things, beginning with humanity, in the crucified and glorified Christ.

With these fundamental premises, we base all our reflections on the conviction that God does not make human beings "homosexual." God makes men and women to live human lives of love through their complementary communion with each other on all levels of human being and life: physical, emotional, spiritual, *and* sexual. Human beings, in this view, become subject to same-sex feelings and desires that are specifically sexual—that is, that seek fulfillment in erotic, genital sexual activities—because of the fallen state of humanity into which they are born and in which they live. Human beings, therefore, are not "homosexual" in the same way that they are men or women, black or white, Asian or African, or a mixture of racial and/or national elements.

While sexuality that may be expressed in properly ordered heterosexual feelings and actions is an essential element in human being and life, sexual desires for carnal relations with persons of one's own sex are not a part of a person's basic sexual identity as a human being. A man with sexual thoughts and feelings for other men is still a male human being, and a woman sexually attracted to women is still a woman. And all men and women, whatever their sexual feelings, proper and improper, are human beings who cannot be essentially defined in their God-given humanity by their feelings and desires—feelings and desires that have been produced in them by their biological, psychological, and cultural inheritance, and by the way they have been treated by others, particularly family members, within the corrupted conditions of the fallen world.[5]

1 In using the expression "same-sex attraction," I follow the example of the Courage movement in the Roman Catholic Church. See Paul Scalia, "A Label that Sticks," *First Things*, June/July 2005, No. 154, pp. 12–14.

2 In the first of his apostolic letters, St. Paul writes to the Thessalonians, "Now may the God of peace Himself sanctify you completely; and may your whole spirit [*pneuma*], soul [*psyche*], and body [*soma*] be preserved blameless at the coming of our Lord Jesus Christ." And he adds, "He who calls you is faithful, who also will do it" (1 Thess. 5:23–24). In English translations of the NT, "spiritual" is sometimes unfortunately translated as "supernatural," and "psychic" as "natural" or even "unspiritual." In some patristic translations, "psychic" is translated as "animal," from the Latin word for soul (*anima*).

3 Sometimes the "image of God" in humans is identified with their spirit, soul, or mind. This is misleading and inaccurate. Humans are made "according to God's image and likeness" to have divine qualities, and so to be and act as God is and acts, in the wholeness of their humanity. To be and act in a divine manner, humans must first of all be spiritual (*pneumatikos, noetikos, logikos*). But they must also be psychic and bodily, in male and female forms. The spirit/*pneuma* (or mind/*nous* or word/*logos*) is to govern a person's soul and body with their emotions and passions (see below). If the "spirit" alone were God's image in creatures, then bodiless powers, i.e. angels, and not human beings, would be made "according to God's image and likeness." We must note here as well that God is not "a spirit." God is completely different (*totaliter aliter*) from creatures in every way. To refer to God as "spirit" is as anthropomorphic as to speak of God's eyes or hands. In St. John's Gospel, Jesus says "God is Spirit" to indicate that God is not located anywhere, and must be worshipped "in spirit and truth" (John 4:24). The Lord here is not making a metaphysical statement about God's being, which, according to the Orthodox church fathers' interpretation of the Bible, as well as their personal mystical experience, is "beyond being [*hyperousios*]" and even "beyond divinity [*hypertheos*]."

4 The Orthodox patristic teaching is that humans, to be truly human, are to be by God's grace (*kata charin theou*), good will (*kat' evdokian*), action (*kat' energeian*), and power (*kata dynamin*) everything that God Himself is by nature (*kat'ousian*). Their creaturely constitution as spiritual, psychic, and bodily beings makes this deification possible.

5 On genetic inheritance and environmental influence in regard to sexuality, see Dean Hamer and Peter Copeland, *Living with Our Genes, Why They Matter More Than You Think* (New York: Doubleday, 1998), especially pp. 158–200. In 1993 Hamer's lab discovered the "so-called gay gene" about which he comments in this book (pp.

182–183). See also V. S. Ramachandran and Sandra Blakeslee, *Phantoms in the Brain, Probing the Mysteries of the Human Mind* (New York: HarperCollins, 1999). Also T. Hopko, *Sin: Primordial, Generational, Personal* [Audio recording] (Crestwood, NY: SVS Press, 1990).

— 5 —

Same-Sex Attraction and Goodness

CHRISTIANITY IN ITS ORTHODOX UNDERSTANDING professes that all creatures (including demons), and certainly all human beings, are good by nature.[1] No one and nothing is evil as such. Evil is always a "parasite" on something good. Evil actions are always someone's misuse and abuse—knowingly or unknowingly, voluntarily or involuntarily—of what is substantially good. And evil people are always human beings who are essentially and basically good in their being made by God.[2]

Unless human beings have completely corrupted their humanity (which, according to Orthodox Christianity, seems to be impossible, since the possibility for repentance is never wholly destroyed), they are, knowingly or unknowingly, hungering and thirsting for what is good, true, and beautiful in everything they do, including their sexual actions.[3] They are seeking satisfaction, fulfillment, comfort, and joy. In Christian terms, they are longing for holiness and union with God, and with all creatures in God.

All human beings, in this understanding, are ordered to God, and will not be satisfied, peaceful, and comforted until they rest in Him.[4] There is no difference here between men and women, whatever their sexual inclinations and desires. When human beings engage in sexual activities—heterosexual or homosexual, intimate or anonymous, committed or casual, proper or improper—whether or not they acknowledge it, they are in fact longing for unending divine life, peace, comfort, and happiness in God. In this sense, they are exercising, albeit often in twisted ways that are doomed to failure, a God-given gift intended to be an expression of and a participation in humanity's communion with God, who is Love.

1 This applies even to C.S. Lewis' "men without chests" who, having lost "the Tao," he argues, are no longer "human" in "the old sense," and, as such, cannot be said to be "good" or "bad." See *The Abolition of Man* (San Francisco: Harper, 2001, originally 1944), p. 163. This little book should be required reading for everyone interested in humanity, and especially human sexuality, in the Western world today. See also Karl Stern, *The Pillar of Fire* (Garden City, NY: Image Books, 1959, first published by Harcourt, Brace and Co., 1951). The author predicts that "once Marxism is finished" humanity is "in for a global experiment" that he calls "rationalist pragmatism" or "scientism," which, he says, will be "the one form of society which is worse than the Marxist or the Fascist one." The eminent scientist and psychologist writes: "Compared with [this 'scientific-technological' society], [Nazi] Germany and [Communist] Russia would look like children's playgrounds. Man's life on this earth would come about as close to the idea of hell as anything on this earth may. [. . .] This, not material destruction, would mean the end of Mankind" (p. 262).

2 For example, St. Maximus the Confessor writes, "The proper use of these [spiritual and psychic] powers produces spiritual knowledge, moral judgment, love and self-restraint. This being so, nothing created and given existence by God is evil. [. . .] This being so, it is only the misuse of things that is evil, and such misuse occurs when the mind (*nous*) fails to cultivate its natural powers." *Third Century on Love:* 3, 4. See T. Hopko, "On God and Evil," in *Abba—The Tradition of Orthodoxy in the West*, Festschrift for Bishop Kallistos Ware (Crestwood, NY: SVS Press, 2003), pp. 179–192.

3 Texts such as Matt. 12:31 (Mark 3:28–30; Luke 12:10); Mark 14:21; 2 Pet. 2:4–22; Jude 6–13 seem to say that human beings can totally lose their humanity. Taking the whole of Scripture, however, it might more accurately be said that human beings can become more and more inhuman, while never losing their basic humanity, which allows them to be everlastingly more sinful and ungodly. In this view, an endless process of *dehumanization* is the evil opposite to an everlasting process of *deification*. See T. Hopko, "On God and Evil" (cited above).

4 St. Augustine's famous line in the beginning of his *Confessions*, 1:1, "You have created us for Yourself, and our heart knows no rest until it rests in You."

— 6 —

Same-Sex Attraction and Passion

FOR ORTHODOX CHRISTIANITY, HUMAN PASSIONS and desires are naturally good.[1] They are an essential part of human nature made by God in His own image and likeness. They belong by necessity to human being and life. They become evil only when they are misdirected and misused.

A passionate desire (*epithymia*) for what is good, true, right, and beautiful is natural and praiseworthy when properly directed by a person's governing faculty (*heguomenikon* or *logistikon*) with freedom (*eleutheria*), self-control (*enkrateia*), and dispassion (*apatheia*).[2] So are passionate feelings for union with others (*eros*) in charity (*agape*), friendship (*philia*), and affection (*storge*). So is passionate zeal (*thymos*) for all that is of God. The Bible testifies that Christ and even God the Father Himself exercise the passionate faculties of desire and zeal in their relationship with creatures.

When human beings misdirect and misuse their God-given faculty of passionate desire (epithymia), it becomes perverted and deformed into the blameworthy passion of sinful lust, which in its specifically sexual expressions is generally called "fornication" (*porneia*) in the New Testament Scriptures and writings of the saints.[3] When this passion in its corrupted condition is repeatedly enacted, which it can be in any number of ways, it becomes addictive and enslaving. Similarly, we may note, when humans misdirect and misuse their God-given faculty of fervent zeal (*thymos*), it is deformed into ungodly anger and rage, which also, when given free

23

reign, become compulsively and obsessively enslaving. Thus the biblical admonition, "Be angry, and do not sin" (Ps. 4:4; Eph. 4:26).

In the traditional Orthodox Christian view, passions that are simply sexual—in the sense that they have nothing to do with love in any of its forms, but are wholly self-centered and exclusively driven by a desire for carnal and emotional pleasure as an end in itself—are always sinful, whether heterosexual or homosexual. They "miss the mark" for which they are given by God. They are originally produced in a person, as are all sinful physical, emotional, intellectual, and spiritual passions, by the ungodly elements in a person's heredity and environment, and by the person being treated in ungodly ways by others. When these sexual passions are acted upon, voluntarily or involuntarily, they lead to personal sins. They render a person *culpable*, however, only to the degree that they are willingly chosen, consciously embraced, and intentionally enacted.[4]

It is crucial to understand at this point that Jesus in the Gospels does not say that people with sinful sexual thoughts and feelings are guilty of sexual sin. This is so, as Christian saints never tire of explaining, because it is virtually impossible not to have such sinful thoughts and feelings in this world's corrupted condition. Jesus rather says that people become guilty of sexual sin when they intentionally look upon others in order to lust after them in ungodly, selfish, and exclusively carnal ways, which is to say, without true and genuine love—and, of course, when they actually act in these ways.[5]

Orthodox Christian Scriptures and saints universally testify that when the attraction between persons of the same sex is godly, genital sexual activity is precluded, because divine love cannot be expressed in sexual intercourse between persons of the same sex. This is so, it is claimed, because same-sex intercourse—however it is enacted, and however committed the persons are to each other, and however "monogamous" their relationship is, and however much they believe that they love each other with godly love—can never be complementary, unitive, life-creating, and life-enhancing in the ways that God intended human sexual intercourse to be between a man and a woman.

Same-sex sexual intercourse is not capable of establishing and edifying the physical, emotional, and spiritual lives of the persons involved. Nor can it express and model human relationships as God intended them to be from the beginning, and as God saved and sanctified them to be in Christ and the Holy Spirit. Christian Scripture claims that those who dishonor their bodies through homosexual intercourse have knowingly or unknowingly "exchanged the truth of God [and about men and women in God's image] for the lie, and worshiped and served the creature rather than the Creator, who is blessed forever" (Rom. 1:24–25).

Love can be faithfully expressed and fruitfully fulfilled in sexual activity, according to Christian Orthodoxy, exclusively in the complementary, unconditional, and life-creating communion between a man and a woman, which Christ exemplifies in His union of love with the Church, with whom He becomes "one flesh" (Eph. 5:21–33). In this view, same-sex attractions that lead to genital sexual activity (like sexual acts between men and women outside—and at times even within—the community of marriage) are betrayals of the love that God is. As such, these acts inevitably end up harming everyone involved, beginning with the couple themselves. And they prevent their practitioners and defenders from having a life of virtue and contemplation in the "union of love" (*henosis agapis*) with God through Christ and the Spirit that begins on earth in the Church's sacramental and spiritual life and endures forever in the age to come.[6]

All this is not to say that all genital sexual activities between people of the same sex (as well as sexual acts between unmarried men and women, and even many married men and women who have little or no relationship with God) are totally devoid of authentic elements of godly love. If such were the case, such actions would be completely demonic and totally destructive, which they obviously, by God's grace and mercy, are not. But it is to say that while sexual intercourse between a man and a woman has the possibility of being a pure and proper actualization of divine love when enacted in a godly manner, homosexual intercourse does not.

Countless people today deny this Orthodox Christian conviction. They claim that sexual activity between people of the same sex has the capability of being as natural, loving, godly, and holy as sexual love between a married man and woman. People who consider themselves Christians, including men and women in ordained ministries in Christian churches, hold this view, with widespread approval. Orthodox Christianity, however, as we have just asserted, has traditionally denied that God can be the cause and content of sexual acts between people of the same sex, as well as between people of opposite sexes who are not married to each other in all aspects of godly love.[7] Or to put it another way, perhaps a bit more accurately, Orthodoxy's Scriptures, sacraments, and saints testify to the conviction that praiseworthy passionate love between people of the same sex is betrayed, and not fulfilled, by genital sexual activity, just as praiseworthy passionate love between people of opposite sexes is betrayed by sexual activity with anyone other than one's spouse.[8] (We will reflect further on this point below.)

Because heterosexual attractions and desires are also confused and deranged in humanity's present condition, and are not at all normal or godly in all instances (and perhaps not even in *most*), I must stress again the traditional Orthodox Christian conviction that the love of a man and a woman has to be what God willed it to be "from the beginning" if it is to be healthy and holy, which is to say, if it is to be divinely loving.[9] That a couple has been legally, even sacramentally, married is no guarantee that this will be so. Many men and women wed in Orthodox churches do not believe what is prayed and signified in the sacrament, nor struggle to actualize it in their daily lives. And many women and men who have not been sacramentally, or perhaps even legally, married may in fact have a truly divine union of sexual love in charity, eros, friendship, and affection. When such is the case, according to the witness of the Church's Scriptures and saints, their union may be truly of God because it is an expression of love that accords with God's law, which is "written in their hearts" (Rom. 2:12–16; also 1 John 4:7–21). (We shall also return to this point later in our reflections.)

1 The word "passion" is used in Christian writings in different ways. Its meaning must be determined by context. The word is used for God-given spiritual, emotional, and bodily "passions" that can be used for good or evil, such as desire, zeal, anger, or grief. More often, however, the word "passion" is used for sinful bodily, carnal, emotional, or spiritual "passions" without a qualifying adjective, or with such qualifiers as *sinful, culpable, unnatural, reprehensible,* or *blameworthy*. The words "desire" (*epithymia*), "world" (*cosmos*), and "flesh" (*sarx*) are also used in different ways that can be understood only in context (e.g. compare John 3:15–16 and 1 John 2:15–17). See also St. Maximus the Confessor's writings published in *The Philokalia*, Volume II, edited by Palmer, Sherrard and Ware (London: Faber and Faber, 1981), with the note on "passion" in the glossary, pp. 385–6. For example, St. Maximus says that "a culpable [in Sherwood's translation 'blameworthy'] passion is an impulse of the soul that is contrary to nature" (*First Century on Love*, 35). See also Bishop Ignatius Brianchaninov (a.k.a. St. Ignatius, or Ignatii, Brianchaninoff), *The Arena: An Offering to Contemporary Monasticism* (Jordanville, NY: Holy Trinity Monastery, 1997, originally published in 1867), chapter 41, "The Meaning of the Term 'World,'" pp. 166–177.

2 In Orthodox spiritual teaching, dispassion (*apatheia*) is not indifference, insensibility, insensitivity, lack of feeling, or absence of receptivity. It is certainly not hardheartedness or contempt. It is rather the freedom and capability not to be acted upon in a harmful manner against one's nature and will. Only a "dispassionate" person can be genuinely compassionate, possessing authentic sympathy and empathy, understood as the ability to be engaged with others without being symbiotically enmeshed in their lives and activities, and to be free from others without being indifferent or contemptuous. Thus Christian Scriptures speak of the free and sinless Christ being "made sin" for us (2 Cor. 5:21) and undergoing His "voluntary Passion," an expression used in Orthodox liturgy, together with such other expressions as Christ's "passionless Passion." Christian saints speak of "dispassionate passion" and "dispassionate compassion" and the "fire of dispassion" and "the passion of deification." They also speak of overcoming passion by passion, eros by eros, desire by desire, and fire by fire. See, for example, St. John Climakos, *The Ladder of Divine Ascent*, and the multivolume collection of writings called the *Philokalia* (for example, those of St. Maximus the Confessor and St. Diodokhos of Photike). For a succinct summary of the patristic teaching on passion and dispassion, see in the *Philokalia,* Kallistos and Ignatios of Xanthopoulos, "Directions to Hesychasts," pp. 86–89.

3 See Matt. 19:9; 1 Cor. 6:13, 18, and others, where *porneia* is translated into English as "sexual immorality," "unchastity," or "fornication." Regarding *porneia* in the writings of the church fathers, see St. John Cassian, "On the Eight Vices" in the *Philokalia*, and "On the Spirit of Porneia," *Institutes*, Bk 6; St. John Climakos, *The Ladder of Divine Ascent*, Step 15; St. Isaac of Syria, *The Ascetical Homilies*, 41; St. Nilus of the Sora (Nil' Sorskii), "The Eight Principal Vices of the Soul" in *The Monastic Rule*; St. Ignatius Brianchaninoff, *The Arena*, chapter 42. Also *The Sayings of the Desert Fathers*, e.g. St. Anthony's word (11) that *porneia* is the one passion with which the monk, even in desert solitude, is never freed from struggle.

4 We must note that in the Orthodox tradition both conditions and actions can be "sinful" without necessarily being "culpable." For example, a child can say and do things, imitating adults, which are objectively sinful but are hardly culpable. Regarding culpability, both as to its presence and degree in a person, God alone is the judge. According to Christ in the Gospels, people who know more and better are judged more severely than people who know poorly or not at all. See Luke 12:41–48; John 13:17. This also is the apostolic teaching, e.g. Rom. 2 and James 4:17. In this view, Orthodox Christians will be judged more severely than all other people. It must also be noted in this regard that according to Orthodox teaching, God's judgment is not "comparative." It cannot be said, for example, that A is "more sinful" than B. God judges each person exclusively on what they know and do according to their unique providence. For this reason each person can and indeed must claim before God to be "the first" of sinners. On this issue see St. Isaac of Syria, *The Ascetical Homilies* (Boston: Holy Transfiguration Monastery, 1984), Homily 9 (e.g. "There are sins which a person commits from weakness, being drawn into them against his will, and there are sins which a person commits voluntarily, and ones from ignorance. Also, it happens that a person will sin due to accidental circumstance, or again, because of his long continuance in evil, or from habit. Although all these modes and kinds of sins are blameworthy, yet with respect to the punishment to be exacted for each, one is found to be comparatively greater than the other. The blame of one sin is very great and its repentance is accepted only with difficulty, but another is more easily forgiven," p. 71).

5 Matt. 5:27–30. Also *The Sayings of the Desert Fathers*, Poemen 15, 20, 28, pp. 142–143.

6 It is a teaching of virtually all philosophies and religions, Hellenistic and Abrahamic as well as Hindu and Buddhist, that sexual activity greatly hinders a life of virtue and spiritual contemplation, and completely prevents it when devoid of "true love," however this is understood.

7 Evidence exists that seems to demonstrate that sinful sexual passions and actions between persons, both heterosexual and homosexual, diminish and often even disappear as godly forms of love grow and deepen in their relationship. Perhaps this is because sexual acts between unmarried people ultimately harm, rather than enhance, their mutual charity, friendship, and affection. Genital sex also seems to diminish and often even to disappear between gay men who remain together in long-term domestic arrange-

ments as they continue to engage in sexual activities with men and boys other than their domestic partners. Some gay men have told me that this is so. I have no information on this subject from lesbians. I see this point being made in Daniel Mendelsohn's autobiographical essay, *The Elusive Embrace, Desire and the Riddle of Identity* (New York: Vintage Books, 2000) and in Humphrey Carpenter's descriptions of the sexual behavior of W. H. Auden, Chester Kallman, Christopher Isherwood, and other homosexual men in *W. H. Auden, A Biography* (Boston: Houghton Mifflin Co, 1981).

8 We may note here an analogy between the issues of same-sex love expressed in homoerotic sexual acts and the ordination of women. Neither homoerotic sexual activity (not to speak of same-sex marriage) nor the ordination of women has ever been affirmed in Orthodox Church history (nor in any "mainline" Christian church until the twentieth century). Proponents of the ordination of women and of homoerotic sexual activity (and marriage) basically claim that only two reasons may explain their absence in Orthodox Church history (and in Christianity generally until the twentieth century). One is that both of these practices were originally accepted and affirmed by Christians (certainly by Jesus), but were later wickedly suppressed by powerful heterosexual males. The other is that neither of these practices was accepted or affirmed, for understandable but unacceptable social and/or cultural reasons. Whatever the case, however, proponents of homosexual erotic activity and the ordination of women both insist that Christians must now accept and affirm both practices. There are, of course, proponents of the ordination of women as bishops and priests in Christian churches who do not hold that same-sex love may be expressed in erotic sexual activities. See T. Hopko, Ed., *Women and the Priesthood*, New and Revised Edition (Crestwood: SVS Press, 1999). It may also be noted at this point that classical Judaism, Islam, Hinduism, and Buddhism have not affirmed homoerotic sexual activity, and that monotheistic, polytheistic, and atheistic religions and societies having nothing to do with Judaism, Christianity, or Islam have been no less "male chauvinist" and "heterosexist" than the religious cultures of "Abrahamic traditions."

9 It seems to me that Christ's reference to "from the beginning" when teaching about marriage and sexuality (Matt. 19:1–12) is not about chronology, but rather about God's intentions and purposes for humankind "from the beginning," which "from the beginning" were rejected and violated.

— 7 —

Same-Sex Attraction and Sin

FOLLOWING THE ENTIRE VIEW (*skopos*) of Scripture and the whole testimony of Church Tradition (and not just selected texts on sexual subjects), Orthodox Christianity holds that all human beings are sinful because their common humanity is "off the track" and "missing the mark."[1] All of Adam and Eve's children are born outside Paradise. They are all now formed "in [fallen Adam's] likeness, after his [distorted] image" (Gen. 5:1–3). They must all apply to themselves the words of the Psalmist: "Behold, I was brought forth in iniquity, / And in sin my mother conceived me" (Ps. 51:5).[2]

Because of the universal corruption of humanity from the beginning and through the generations, every person's humanity is sinful and mortal. This includes even those who, by divine grace and the providential blessing of a healthy inheritance and holy environment, may actually sin very little (or perhaps even not at all, as some Christians believe is the case with Christ's Mother Mary). How people actually sin depends on how they deal with the degree and kind of human sinfulness which they inherit and to which others have subjected them through no original fault of their own.[3]

According to Orthodoxy, having involuntary and inculpable sinful desires for sexual activities that are not personally chosen, including passionate feelings for sexual union with persons of one's own sex, is but one of the countless ways that people experience the results of sin in a deformed humanity. And acting on these passions is but one of the many ways that human beings personally sin themselves, with God alone judging their culpability. Resisting these passionate desires by God's grace, or, perhaps more accurately, recognizing their source, refusing to act on them, and redirecting the goodness in them to its proper end—that is, to divine love and to God Himself—is the way that human beings become holy and godlike.

A difficult and delicate point we must consider in our reflections on same-sex attraction and sin is that the paradigmatic "sinner" in Orthodox Christian tradition, following the Bible, is not the "macho man" or the "perverted homosexual." It is the "fallen woman." This seems to be so for at least two reasons. The first is that the Bible uses nuptial and conjugal imagery for God's relation with creation, Yahweh's relation with Israel, and Christ's relation with the Church. In prophetic and apocalyptic writings, the faithless among God's people are likened to "adulterous wives" and "harlots" who "fornicate" with false gods "like lusty stallions" on every high place and under every green tree, as they sacrifice God's sons and daughters to idols.[4] In the poetic imagery of sacred Scripture, only "virgins," those who are totally faithful to the Lord, having no other gods, enter God's kingdom and participate in "the marriage supper of the Lamb." They alone are "the bride of the Lamb" everlastingly adorned in divine beauty (Rev. 14:4–5, and others).

The point here is that the infidelity of God's people to their Lord is likened in the Bible to a wife's infidelity to her husband. Thus we have the "adulterous wife" and the "harlot" as the central symbol in Christian Scripture and tradition for the general sinfulness of humanity (*anthropos*) toward God, who is its divine "Husband" and "Lord."

Another reason the "woman fallen in sin" may be the predominant symbol of the general sinfulness of humanity in classical Christian tradition is the indispensable ministry that women have for human holiness, through what they alone can provide for humanity—beginning with their husbands and children if they are married, and for human beings generally, whether or not they are married. The stories in Genesis, particularly as they are appropriated and interpreted by the New Testament writers and Christian authors of later generations, seem to support such an explanation.

The clear testimony of the biblical story of creation is that Adam alone is not Man (*anthropos*). "Man," or as we say today, "humanity," is man and woman together: "male and female He created them" (Gen. 1:27). The well-being of humanity requires the complementary communion of male and female, in which, according to the second creation story in Genesis, the woman's task *as woman* is to be the "helper comparable" to man, for whom it "is not good [to] be alone" (Gen. 2:18). Thus, when women reject their specifically womanly calling for the sake of the common humanity of men and women together, or when they are unable or unwilling to provide their specifically womanly gifts because of the wounds inflicted upon them by sinful men (who have renounced or corrupted their masculine "headship" as imaged in God's love for Israel and Christ's love for the Church), they are viewed as the foremost symbol of human sinfulness. The "sinful woman," in this regard, stands as the prime example that humanity (*anthropos*) as a whole, male and female together, is truly "fallen."

Orthodox Church tradition makes this same point in reverse, so to speak, in its conviction that the most perfect human being, who images and symbolizes the holiness of humanity (*anthropos*) as a whole in its relationship to God and Christ, is a woman, not a man. She is, of course, Christ's Virgin Mother Mary, the all-holy Theotokos, who by faith and grace in keeping God's commandments is wholly deified.[5]

All this is not at all to say that all men and women must be married. Nor is it to say that women find and fulfill themselves solely in serving as conjugal "helpmates" for their husbands and heads. It is to say, however, that men and women belong together and need each other for their mutual fulfillment and sanctity, whether or not they are married. And it is also to say that all men, married and unmarried, need women in order to fulfill their humanity made in God's image, male and female, as, in turn, all women also need men. The lives of the Christian saints, both men and women, the majority of whom were unmarried, convincingly demonstrate this point.[6]

Although the "homosexual" is not the symbolically paradigmatic "sinner" in Christian tradition, it is surely true that sexual desires and actions among people of the same sex are presented in Christian writings as striking examples of the effects of ancestral, generational, and personal sin in human being and life.[7] The opening lines of St. Paul's letter to the Romans emphatically make this point. After claiming that humans have become futile in their thinking, with darkened hearts and minds, because of their unwillingness to acknowledge "His [God's] invisible attributes [*ta aorata theou*] . . . even His eternal power [*dynamis*] and Godhead [*theotes*]" and their refusal to "glorify" (*edoxasan*) and "thank" (*eucharistisan*) God, the apostle continues:

> For this reason God gave them up to vile passions. For even their women exchanged the natural use for what is against nature. Likewise also the men, leaving the natural use of the woman, burned in their lust for one another, men with men committing what is shameful, and receiving in themselves the penalty of their error which was due. And even as they did not like to retain God in their knowledge, God gave them over to a debased mind, to do those things which are not fitting. (Rom. 1:26–28)

We must emphasize once more that, according to Orthodox Christianity, having loving desires for people of one's own sex is not at all sinful; it is perfectly natural, normal, and necessary. Having lustful thoughts and feelings of a purely sexual nature for others, however, whether heterosexual or homosexual, is unnatural, abnormal, and sinful. This should not, however, produce the fear, anxiety, shame, and guilt that it often does in those who have such thoughts, desires, and feelings—which is virtually all of us—because we have them for the most part through no choice or fault of our own. It is ridiculous, therefore, and truly abominable when sinful people whose voluntary and involuntary sins cause, condition, and contribute to the sins of others (especially their children) blame, shame, and punish people (including their children) for what enters their minds, hearts, emotions, and senses simply because they have been born, raised, and compelled to live in a corrupted world.

Although such thoughts and feelings may come to us through no fault of our own, we nevertheless have the ability and responsibility in Christ to take captive such thoughts (2 Cor. 10:5) and redirect such feelings. According to Orthodox Christianity, human beings have the ability to discover and name the causes of their sinful thoughts and feelings. They can engage in ascetic and therapeutic activities that uproot and diminish the enslaving power of such feelings. They can avoid sensing and thinking about things that produce and strengthen those feelings in ways that lead to actual sin. Indeed, they have countless means at their disposal to deal with the sinful thoughts and feelings that come to them unwilled and unwanted.[8]

The tragic truth, however, is that countless people, especially in contemporary secularized societies, have become convinced that their sinful thoughts and feelings, including, and even especially, those having to do with sex, are perfectly normal and natural and, as such, define who they are in their essential being and life. They therefore see no purpose or need in resisting, disciplining, and ultimately destroying them. They are convinced, on the contrary, that to do so would be dishonest, would be to deny and destroy themselves as persons, and, as such, would result in their personal death, which, according to Christian Orthodoxy, is the exact opposite of the truth.

1 The literal meaning of the word sin (*hamartia* in Greek) is to "miss the mark." All words and symbols for evil testify to the basic goodness of things. Missing the mark presupposes the mark. Deviation presupposes a way. Fall presupposes a state from which one falls. Impurity and uncleanness testify to what was pure and clean. Alienation and estrangement witness to a home or homeland where one is no longer found. Transgression includes the notion of a norm or law that has been broken or violated. Rebellion witnesses to the existence of that which is rebelled against. Corruption signifies a disintegration of what was once whole and healthy.

2 This verse does not say that humans are conceived in sins and brought forth in iniquities (plural in the Septuagint) because they are procreated by sexual intercourse. It rather says that by being conceived and born in a fallen world by sinful people, all humans are inevitably affected and infected by the sins of their progenitors and their fellow creatures, over which they have no control and for which they are not personally guilty. See T. Hopko, *Sin: Primordial, Generational and Personal* [Audio Cassette] (Crestwood, NY: SVS Press, 1992).

3 Fr. Alexander Schmemann often said that human life (and so "Christian spirituality") are only about "how you deal with what you've been dealt." Following the classical Christian teachers, he also emphasized that this is different for every person, and that this is all the Lord cares about when He judges our behavior.

4 Is. 1—2; Jer. 2—3; Ezek. 16; Hosea; Rev. 17, and others. According to the Bible, humanity's basic sin is not atheism. It is idolatry. In this perspective, all people have their god. It is either a god (or gods) that they have made or others have inflicted upon them, which they command and control; or it is the God who made them, whom they are commanded to worship and obey for their own good. In this view, there are no atheists, but only idolaters. This is a point of frequent commentary and reflection in patristic writings.

5 See T. Hopko, *Mary: Icon of Human Perfection* [Video Cassette] (Crestwood, NY: SVS Press, 1992). It is common in the Orthodox Christian tradition from the post-apostolic age to see Mary as the "new Eve" with Christ as the "new Adam."

6 Saints tend to come in clusters of men and women together, often parents, children, and siblings. We note not only Jesus, His Mother Mary, and His women disciples led by Mary Magdalene, but the great Cappadocian saints Basil the Great, Gregory of Nyssa, and Gregory the Theologian with the two Macrinas, Emmelia, Nonna, Theosoebia, and Gorgonia. We may also note outstanding spiritual couples in Christian history, such as John Chrysostom and the widowed deaconess Olympia in the East, and Francis and Clare, John of the Cross and Teresa of Avila, in the West. Note may also be made of the special spiritual relationships that St. Seraphim of Sarov and St. Nektarios of Aegina had with the nuns with whom they lived and worked. See T. Hopko, *God and Gender* and *Gender and Sanctity* [Audio tapes] (Crestwood, NY: SVS Press, n.d.).

7 Some biblical interpreters, including eminent members of the Orthodox Church, argue that verses 18 to 32 of Romans 1 have nothing to do with what they call "natural

theology" and what I call "ancestral and generational sin." I disagree with them. I believe that the apostle is precisely describing what went wrong with humanity "ever since the creation of the world" and why people have been given over to ignorance and idolatry, and so are unable to recognize the Scriptures and Christ Himself as the Word of God. I also believe that high among the errors of Christian thinking is a wrong formulation of the issue of "natural" and "supernatural," leading to a false dichotomy and opposition between what is "natural" and what is "revealed" and what can be "naturally known" and what is "divinely revealed," ultimately resulting in the false dichotomy between nature and grace, faith and reason, belief and knowledge. These false dichotomies have caused countless difficulties for countless people.

8 "Abba Anoub asked Abba Poemen about impure thoughts which the heart of man brings forth and about vain desires. Abba Poemen said to him, 'Is the axe any use without someone to cut with it? [Is 10:15]. If you do not make use of these thoughts [and desires] they will be ineffectual too.'" *The Sayings of the Desert Fathers*, Poemen, 15. Also "A brother came to see Abba Poemen and said to him, 'Abba, I have many thoughts [and feelings] and they put me in danger.' The old man led him outside and said to him, 'Expand your chest and do not breathe in.' He said, 'I cannot do that.' Then the old man said to him, 'If you cannot do that, no more can you prevent thoughts [and feelings] from arising, but you can resist them.'" Poemen, 28. See also Poemen 14, 21, 59, 62, 140, 154, 176. See also the disconcerting saying of John the Dwarf, 13.

— 8 —

Same-Sex Attraction and Choice

IN THE GOSPEL NARRATIVES, Jesus often asks the question, "What do you want?" According to Orthodoxy, the Lord asks this same question in one way or another of all human beings. The answer to Christ's question for Christians, Orthodoxy clearly contends, must always be the same. It has to be, "I want whatever You want for me."

According to Orthodoxy, as we have been saying, human beings do not choose their sexual feelings and predispositions. They can, however, choose to accept and act on them, or to resist and reject them when the feelings are sinful. Humans can choose to affirm their feelings, or work to diminish and destroy their destructive power. They can choose to live by God's love, employing every means God provides for their healing, or they can choose death (Deut. 30:15–20).

We must also remind ourselves that people may choose to act willingly, and do things willfully, without great passion or compulsion. For example, people with basically heterosexual feelings and passions may simply decide to have a "homosexual experience." They may engage in sexual activities with persons of their own sex not because of compelling predispositions or irresistible attractions. They may do so for purely willful and voluntary reasons, such as curiosity, boredom, rebellion, vindictiveness, hatred, hostility, the desire for sexual pleasure, or the will to make a political statement.

When reflecting on the idea of choice, we must also consider another conviction of Orthodox Christian faith that is relevant to same-sex attraction and love. I ask my readers to be especially patient in their efforts to understand what I am trying to say here.

According to Orthodox Christian doctrine, there is a sense in which human beings do not really have choices about anything at all. We do not have choices about our feelings and passions, as I have repeatedly claimed, because we simply have the feelings that we do (unless we do things to bring them on or stir them up). And as creatures of God, certainly as believers and Christians, we also do not have choices about our purely voluntary actions. This is because we understand ourselves as bound to obey God's will in all things. In this understanding, the root of actual, personal sin is not in making bad choices. It is rather in the presumption that we human beings have choices at all, and in thinking and acting as if we do.

Jesus is the best example of the subtle and difficult point I am now trying to make. It is a dogma of the Orthodox Church that Jesus never chose anything except to do the will of His Father, and even this was not really a "choice" because it involved no deliberation.[1] Because Jesus was perfectly free in His perfect love and knowledge of truth, and His perfect obedience to the Father, He freely willed and spontaneously accomplished the Father's will in all things. In this sense, it can be said that the Lord never did anything by His own choice. Or, put another way, Jesus' only choice in all things was to do God's will, which, in this sense, amounts to having no "choices" at all. Governed by the Holy Spirit in complete communion with God His Father and, as such, being totally free and wholly illumined, Jesus turned from evil and chose the good from His earliest childhood. He could not do otherwise. In this sense, one cannot imagine Jesus "deciding" or "choosing" anything. Nor can one imagine a real believer in God doing so.[2]

Following this way of thinking and speaking, faithful people do not "choose" their professions or determine their actions, including how they will act sexually. They do not "choose" to be a priest or a plumber, for example, or to be celibate or married, or to act or not act on their sexual feelings and desires, heterosexual or homosexual. They know that though they can try to choose to be and do whatever they want, and are being urged to do so from every side, they may not do so. They rather consider themselves compelled by God's love to be and to act in certain ways and to do certain things. They see themselves as having no options other than to obey God's will in all things, trusting in His guidance to lead them and counting on His mercy when they willingly or unwillingly err.

Faithful people order their lives according to this understanding in every possible way. They pray, fast, give alms, and participate in liturgical worship. They read Scripture and other spiritual books. They observe the behavior of others and take counsel from wise people. They engage in therapeutic programs in order to deal with their history, to name the causes of their disease and discontent, and to take responsibility for their behavior, as God would have them do. And they do all these things, and whatever else they find helpful, for this one purpose only. They want to do God's will in the smallest, seemingly most insignificant details of their everyday existence in this fallen world, because they are convinced that this is the only way they will find freedom, happiness, fulfillment, and life for themselves and those they love (Luke 16:10; 19:17).

---

1 The Church's teaching defined at the Sixth Ecumenical Council, following St. Maximus the Confessor and those with him, is that Jesus had the natural human will (*thelyma physikon*) that belongs to human nature. He was a real human being. But, being perfectly free and in unbroken communion with God, Jesus had no deliberative will (*thelyma gnomikon*). This means, in our terms, that He did no "choosing." In this understanding of things, unlike our modern American view, the freer a person is, the less they choose. Thus a person who would be perfectly free by God's grace would never "choose" anything at all. They would see, know, and will what is good, true, and beautiful, and do it. Like Jesus in Gethsemane, they would literally "have no choice," even when they would wish that things could be otherwise.

2 See John 8:31ff; Rom. 6:12–19; 2 Cor. 3:17; throughout Gal. 4—5; James 1:25.

— 9 —

Same-Sex Attraction and God's Will

I BELIEVE THAT ORTHODOX CHRISTIANITY, with its understanding of the biblical testimony, affirms that God's will has two inseparable aspects, which may be called God's *essential goodwill* and God's *providential permission.*[1]

According to Orthodoxy, God *essentially* wills that human beings should grow in divine being and life forever. In this sense, God does not will sickness, suffering, or death for His human creatures. He wills them only the life, health, and happiness that come with their being in communion with Him. Only Christ, the sinless "Man from heaven," who has voluntarily "become sin" for our salvation, has perfectly accomplished God's original, ultimate, and essential goodwill for humanity.[2] Some human beings, however, both before and after the Incarnation of God's Son and Word as Israel's Messiah, have achieved high degrees of holiness, first among whom for Orthodoxy is Jesus' Mother Mary. This is true even of some who have not consciously known Christ, or have never heard the Gospel, as we said above, because they follow God's law "written in their hearts."

The perfect life that God wills for human beings, beginning in this age and enduring forever, is a life of love enacted in perfect truth (*alitheia*), freedom (*eleutheria*), chastity (*sophrosyne*), self-control (*enkrateia*), and dispassion (*apatheia*). It is a life of charity (*agape*), which is love as willing and acting for the good of the other. It is a life of friendship (*philia*), which is love as enjoying the blessings of another's presence in a variety of mutually life-enhancing

43

ways. It is a life of affection (*storge*), understood as tender feeling and emotional attraction—love in the sense of "liking" someone or something. And it is a life of vital and vivifying union (*eros*), which is love as communion with the other in a dynamic and passionate joining of charity, friendship, and affection.[3] All love that fully resembles, imitates, and participates in God's divine love contains all these forms of love, the foremost of which is *agape*, which ensures the divine character and quality of the other three.

According to Orthodoxy, as we have already said, sexual intercourse between faithfully committed men and women may be expressive of divine love, but it also may not be.[4] Sexual intercourse between people of the same sex, however, is incapable of expressing divine love because of the incapability of human beings of the same sex to be sexually united in a mutually fulfilling, complementary, life-creating, and life-enhancing manner. In a word, same-sex attraction resulting in same-sex intercourse, however enacted, is a betrayal of the love God wills for His people.

God's *providential permission* always accompanies God's *essential goodwill* for humanity.

According to Orthodoxy, God knew from all eternity that human beings would refuse to acknowledge His power and divinity in creation and so to give Him the glory and gratitude that are His due. God's *providential permission*, therefore, includes human rebellion and corruption. It includes the most egregious and outrageous forms of evil and injustice. It includes sickness, suffering, and death, culminating, ultimately, in the crucifixion of God's beloved Son Jesus for the world's salvation. And it includes human sexual passions and actions in the flawed forms in which we now know them, both heterosexual and homosexual, in ourselves and in those around us.

In this perspective, sexual thoughts, feelings, and desires for persons of one's own sex, as well as their acceptance and enactment, are part of God's *providential permission* for some people within our disordered humanity. They are not part of God's *essential goodwill*.

Such passions and actions can be said to be "from God" in the sense that God made human beings knowing what they would desire and do. In this sense, *and in this sense only*, can it be said that homosexuality is "God's will" for some people.[5]

It is more accurately said that because of human failings, same-sex desires and passions of a purely sexual nature are "allowed" or "permitted" by God, rather than positively "willed" by Him. As such, same-sex attractions are to be acknowledged and accepted as a most significant (though hardly exclusive) element in the battle in which some people are providentially called to glorify God and save their souls.

In this view, same-sex attraction in its fallen form, which includes desires for genital sexual actions with persons of one's own sex, is a providential cross to be borne and not a divine gift to be celebrated. In saying this, we hasten to reaffirm the conviction that same-sex love, when properly experienced and purely expressed, is always God's sacred gift. Such love is a necessary, normal, and natural part of God's *essential goodwill* for humanity. When such love is missing or violated, voluntarily or involuntarily, it results in same-sex desires that must be acknowledged and dealt with as part of God's *providential permission* for those who have them.

When same-sex love is pure and godly, it grows, blossoms, and is ultimately fulfilled in God's coming kingdom, when humanity will finally attain to "the measure of the stature of the fullness of Christ" (Eph. 4:13). In the new humanity of the new age, all human beings will "know the love of Christ" and "be filled with all the fullness of God" (Eph. 3:19). They will not engage in genital sexual activity of any kind. Being "sons of God" and "sons of the resurrection," they will live like the "angels of God in heaven" (Luke 20:34–36; Matt. 22:30).[6]

1 See St. John of Damascus, *On the Orthodox Faith*, Book 2, chapter 29. St. John uses the terms "antecedent" for what God positively wills for us (what I call God's

essential goodwill) and "consequent" for what God permits as a "concession to free-will" (what I call God's *providential permission*).

2 See 1 Cor. 15:42–50; 2 Cor. 5:16–21; Heb. 2:14–18; 4:14–16; 5:1–10.

3 C. S. Lewis analyzes these distinct forms of love in *The Four Loves* (New York: Harcourt, Inc., 1991).

4 When teaching summer school at the Tibetan Buddhist Naropa Institute in Colorado, I was asked if, according to Orthodoxy, purity, peace, attention, mindfulness, and enlightenment were possible for people during sexual intercourse (which according to traditional Buddhism they are not, a teaching highly debated at that time at Naropa). I said that I thought it was extremely rare, since most sexual acts, even in marriage, are defiled by sins of all kinds (selfishness, lewdness, forgetfulness of the other, sheer carnal pleasure, etc.). I added, however, that according to Orthodoxy it has happened at least twice: in the conception of John the Baptist by Zachariah and Elizabeth, and in the conception of Jesus' Mother Mary by Joachim and Anna. These acts of sexual intercourse are both liturgical feasts in the Orthodox Church, with hymns to be sung and icons to be venerated. Orthodoxy, it may be noted, does not accept the Latin teaching that God had exceptionally to apply the "merits of Christ" beforehand to these acts in order to make them "immaculate," i.e. free from the "stain of original sin" that is allegedly transmitted through acts of procreation by sexual intercourse.

5 My personal view is that the Bible speaks of God's providential activity as being His *will* in the sense that God *willed* to have a world in which creatures corrupt His good creation. He *willed* to make angels who He knew would make themselves demons. And He willed to make human beings who He knew would deform their humanity and that of their children and neighbors, and who would corrupt the world as a whole. God knew all this and did it anyway. In doing so, the Lord decided to use wicked creatures, both human and demonic, as well as evil acts and events, for His beneficent providential purposes. I believe that theologians (especially those of Greek and Latin cultures) use the verbs "allow" and "permit" for what God providentially wills so that no one would think that God personally wills and causes evil, which, of course, He does not. See T. Hopko, "On God and Evil," cited above, pp. 179–192.

6 Being "like angels [*hos angeloi*]" does not mean becoming bodiless. Neither does it mean ceasing to be men and women. It rather means that human beings will cease marrying, reproducing, and living in family units. Jesus says in the Gospels that the "sons of this age marry and are given in marriage [or perhaps more literally, have sex and are given to having sex]. But those who are counted worthy to attain that age, and the resurrection of the dead, neither marry nor are given in marriage; nor can they die anymore, for they are equal to the angels [*isangeloi*] and are sons of God, being sons of the resurrection" (Luke 20:34–36). Jesus gives this teaching in response to the question about which husband gets the woman who has had several husbands on earth as his wife in God's kingdom. In this teaching we see that the sexual intercourse that God willed for married men and women "from the beginning" does not continue forever in "the age of the resurrection."

— 10 —

Same-Sex Attraction and Sanctity

ACCORDING TO ORTHODOXY, Christians with same-sex attractions who believe in God as known and worshipped in the Church, like all Christian believers, will thank God for the providential crosses given to them, however unbearable they seem to be. They will understand that, given who they are in their relationships with others in the actual circumstances of their lives, things could not be different for them from what they are. These Christians will accept this fact and deal with it by every possible means. They will seek help wherever they can find it as they struggle by God's grace to transform their cross into a victory of goodness, beauty, and truth, and a triumph of divine love in their lives.

Millions of people today reject the teaching that same-sex attraction with a yearning for genital sexual activity is a part only of God's *providential permission* for some people, caused and conditioned by sin. They judge such a position to be scandalously ignorant and evil. Some contemporary thinkers, including women and men recognized as Christian theologians, claim that powerful heterosexist men invented and enforced this understanding in order to keep all "others" (especially women) under their control and subjugation. They insist that this doctrine has nothing to do with Jesus' own teaching. To accept the Orthodox Christian view, they therefore insist, is to reject God's *essential goodwill* for human beings. It is to reject divine love, truth, and justice, and so to reject Jesus Himself.[1]

47

It must nevertheless be emphasized once more that people with same-sex attractions who profess Christian faith in the Orthodox way will accept their homosexual desires as their cross—as a providential part of their struggle to glorify God and save their lives in a sinful world. They will view their same-sex attractions as a crucial part of their God-given path to sanctity and deification, both for themselves and for the people around them, particularly their families and potential sexual partners. And they will see their refusal to act out their feelings sexually as an extraordinary opportunity for imitating Christ and participating in His saving Passion. They will, in a word, take up their erotic sexual desires, with their desire to love and be loved, as an essential part of their personal striving to fulfill St. Paul's appeal:

> I beseech you therefore, brethren, by the mercies of God, that you present your bodies a living sacrifice, holy, acceptable to God, *which is* your reasonable service. And do not be conformed to this world, but be transformed by the renewing of your mind, that you may prove what is that good and acceptable and perfect will of God. (Rom. 12:1–2)

The way of sanctity for heterosexuals and homosexuals alike includes the way in which they deal with the effects of ancestral and generational sin in their lives, as well as with all the sins that have been committed against them from their earliest days on earth, and even from before they were born. It also involves dealing with the effects of one's own personal sins and failings, especially those committed in early life. It demands that one deal bravely and honestly with one's history, family, religion, culture, and nation. It requires painful remembering, blessed mourning, sincere forgiving, ceaseless praying, and the courageous acceptance of one's providential destiny caused and conditioned by sin. It demands a firm and unwavering resolve to take full responsibility before God for one's desires and actions. It also demands heartfelt forgiveness of those who have voluntarily or involuntarily hurt and harmed one. The way of sanctity, therefore, is not a resignation to one's fate; it is the ascetical transformation of one's being and life by God's grace and power.

1 See Robert Goss, *Jesus Acted Up, A Gay and Lesbian Manifesto* (HarperSanFrancisco, 1993) and Carter Heyward, *Touching Our Strength, The Erotic Power and the Love of God* (HarperSanFrancisco, 1989) for views that identify God with erotic power and propose gay and lesbian experiences of erotic love as a model for the liberation of all people from the evils of patriarchal heterosexist domination. Among Goss' goals, following the method of Charles Foucault, are to "recover the dangerous memories of Jesus and biblical truth from their heterosexist system of discursive practice," to have "Christology . . . liberated from a pseudouniversal discursive practice and recontextualized to the experience of gay and lesbian people," and to see "the Bible . . . rescued from fundamentalism" and become "an empowering resource for gay/lesbian resistance." *Jesus Acted Up*, p. 183. See also the commentaries of Elizabeth Stuart, herself a lesbian theologian, on the views of Goss and Heyward in *Gay and Lesbian Theologies, Repetitions with Critical Differences* (Burlington, VT: Ashgate, 2003). I recommend the writings of Stuart, Heyward, and Goss, with those of Andrew Sullivan, John Boswell, and Virginia Ramey Mollenkott, as most helpful in understanding an affirmation of homosexuality by those who consider themselves, in one way or another, Christians. I also recommend *The Vatican and Homosexuality, Reactions to the "Letter to the Bishops of the Catholic Church on the Pastoral Care of Homosexual Persons,"* edited by Jeannine Gramick and Pat Furey (New York: Crossroad, 1988) as most profitable for understanding different Christian opinions on this issue. In this volume, the essay by Fr. Benedict M. Ashley, "Compassion and Homosexual Orientation" (pp. 105–111), is the best brief essay on this subject that I know of.

— 11 —

Same-Sex Attraction and Asceticism

ASCETIC STRUGGLE IS ESSENTIAL TO CHRISTIAN FAITH and life in this world. Men and women with same-sex attractions, like all who seek life in God, will necessarily be committed to ascetic activities. They will engage in their ascetic exercises, as all must do, under the guidance of experienced elders and with the help of whatever psychological means and therapeutic programs are available to them for this purpose. For, indeed, without such help and support, many people, especially in our present human conditions, will be unable to engage in ascetic practices in fruitful and life-giving ways. They will rather misuse and abuse asceticism because of their woundedness and lack of discernment. For, as St. Anthony the Great already noted in the fourth century: "Some have afflicted their bodies by asceticism, but they lack discernment, and so they are far from God."[1]

First of all, Christians with same-sex attractions will ceaselessly pray, as all Christians must, in all the ways God provides. They will participate in liturgical worship in church. They will practice personal prayer in their rooms. And they will devote themselves to unceasing prayer in their minds and hearts. They will also engage in spiritual reading. They will constantly read the Bible, especially the Psalms and New Testament writings, with the lives and teachings of Christian saints. They will practice silence, both exterior and interior. They will fast and practice periodic abstinence from certain foods. They will guard their senses. They will work in wholesome occupations for the good of others and engage in wholesome

51

bies essential to their own well-being. They will share their possessions with others, especially those poorer than themselves and those in special need. They will also support the Church's missionary, philanthropic, and pastoral work. They will discipline their bodies with vigils and prostrations.

In addition, these Christians will do whatever it takes to control their carnal, emotional, and spiritual lusts. They will "crucify the flesh with its passions and desires" in order not to "fulfill" its "lust" (Gal. 5:16–24). They will "put to death your members which are on the earth: fornication [*porneia*], uncleanness, passion, evil desire, and covetousness, which is idolatry." They will do this in order to "put off the old man [*anthropos,* humanity] with his deeds" and to "put on the new man [*anthropos*] who is renewed in knowledge according to the image of Him who created him" (Col. 3:5–10).[2] And when doing all this, such Christians will never forget that their ascetic practices are not ends in themselves, nor are they "spiritual life" as such. They are but *means*: essential, necessary, and God-given means, but nevertheless only *means* to the end, which is life in communion with God through keeping His commandments.[3]

Those who practice asceticism for the sake of virtue will surely come to know that they will be tested to their last breath. They will be tempted to give up, to give in, and to act in ways contrary to God's will for His creatures. Together with their families and friends, they will endure God's providential will for them in the sinful world. They will trust that they will never be tried beyond their strength, as God promises and provides.[4] In a word, they will do what all those afflicted by the sins of the world must do in order to be divinely human by God's grace and power. They will use every available means to come to love God and their fellow humans and, indeed, the whole of creation, with the love given to them through Christ in the Holy Spirit. They will do the things that empower their labors to love everyone and everything as God in Christ has loved them.[5]

Most important of all, Christians struggling with same-sex attractions that can lead to sin will never lose heart, nor surrender their heart to anyone or anything but God. They will remain in and with Christ in all things, being crucified with Him that they might live with Him. They will resist advice and arguments about human behavior based solely on personal feelings, subjective experiences, and behavioral sciences offered to them by people who have largely (if not wholly) lost the basic intuitions of reality that God has implanted in human hearts to guide and govern human thinking, feeling, and sensing.[6] They will not be deceived by those who analyze humanity in its present condition and offer counsel for human living according to their often accurate but largely irrelevant observations and conclusions.[7] In a word, again, they will not accept the conviction that this *fallen* world is the normal, natural, and necessary gift of God's essential goodwill for His human creatures.

1 Anthony the Great, *The Sayings of the Desert Fathers*, 8.

2 This last line from Colossians is quoted in the prayer for the sanctification of the water at the Orthodox rite of baptism.

3 This point is repeated over and again in St. Ignatius of Brianchaninoff's book *The Arena*. Also in St. Seraphim of Sarov's *Conversation with N. Motovilov*.

4 1 Cor. 10:13; 2 Cor. 12:5–10.

5 John 15:9–17; 1 John 3:11–18; 4:7–21.

6 See note 29 above in reference to C. S. Lewis' teaching in *The Abolition of Man* about the loss of "the Tao" in human beings, which leads inexorably to the annihilation of their humanity, which consists in their ability to recognize, admire, honor, and conform to what is good, true, right, and beautiful in themselves and their world. I again urge those interested in the issue of sexuality today to study this little book.

7 In *Homosexuality: A Freedom Too Far* (Phoenix, AZ: Adam Margrave Books, 1955), C. W. Socarides analyzes the gradual acceptance of homosexuality in American life and institutions. He writes that "a great deal of intelligence can be invested in ignorance when the need for illusion is deep" (p. 234). Some people, of course, make precisely this charge against Orthodox Christians.

— 12 —

Same-Sex Attraction and Scripture

REGULAR READING, STUDY, AND REFLECTION on God's Word in the Bible is an essential part of Christian ascetic life. Believers who fail to be regularly nourished by the "bread of life" become spiritually sick and weak, and eventually they die.[1] According to the Christian saints, the greatest cause of human evil and misery is the ignorance of God's Word. This ignorance is also the main cause of heresy, schism, and sin in the churches.[2] It not only allows the carnal passions of gluttony, fornication (*porneia*), and greed to take root and flourish in people's lives, leading to ungodly anger, sadness, and despondency; but it is also the main reason for the spiritual passions of legalism, ritualism, ungodly zeal, vainglory, and pride that captivate religious people, especially those given to ecclesiastical activism and graceless asceticism.[3]

Ignorance of Scripture is also the ultimate cause of the most destructive of all human enslavements, according to Orthodox Christianity, which is theological, spiritual, and moral delusion (in Greek, *plane*; in Slavonic, *prelest*). This is the condition in which people think they are zealous, righteous, holy, and godly, and even charismatic and prophetic, but are really in the power of their own will and the will of their human and demonic deceivers.[4]

In Orthodox Christian tradition, the Bible is read critically, with intellectual and spiritual discernment. Believers use all available linguistic, literary, historical, and archeological information to illumine the sacred texts. But such study is insufficient to produce a full, deep, and accurate understanding of God's Word. Believers pray for divine enlightenment and direction when reading the Scriptures.[5] They seek guidance in the writings and lives of the church fathers and saints, and they follow the theological interpretations and practical applications of the Bible defined and demanded by the Church's councils and canons. Trained and tested pastors and teachers help them to apply these teachings and canons to contemporary issues.

Orthodox Christians read each line of Scripture in its context and in the light of the Bible as a whole. They read the Old Testament in the light of the New, seeing "the law" as a "tutor" (*pedagogos*) leading to Christ, who removes "the veil" that has covered its deepest meaning until His coming (Gal. 3:24–25; 2 Cor. 3:12–18). They find the "substance" and truth of all the Scriptures in the risen Christ, who "opens their minds" to show how "all things must be fulfilled which were written in the Law of Moses and the Prophets and the Psalms concerning" Him (Col. 2:17; Heb. 10:1; Luke 24:26–49).

Biblical texts relevant to same-sex passions and actions are interpreted in this way.[6] The story of Sodom and Gomorrah, for example, is understood to be not only about violence, rape, and the degradation of strangers; it is also understood, already in apostolic Christian writings, to be about sexual perversion and immorality (Gen. 18—19; 2 Pet. 2:4, Jude 7). Also, the Mosaic laws that forbid sexual intercourse between people of the same sex, together with adultery, fornication, incest, rape, and sexual acts with beasts, can hardly be interpreted as being about "ritual purity" and thus abrogated by Christ.[7] Christian tradition has, in fact, always taught that exactly the opposite is true. The crucified and risen Christ demands a righteousness and perfection from His disciples far beyond the requirements of the old pedagogical laws with their condescension to human weakness and hardness of heart.[8] "For I say to you," Jesus declares, "that unless your righteousness exceeds the righteousness of the scribes and Pharisees, you will by no means enter the kingdom of heaven" (Matt. 5:20).[9]

The most direct reference to homosexuality in the New Testament, as we have seen, is in St. Paul's letter to the Romans, where erotic sexual actions between people of the same sex are used as a striking example of the distortion of human being and life resulting from man's rebellion against God and nature—that is, against the way God made things. An interpretation of this passage that claims the apostle was right in forbidding acts "contrary to nature," but was ignorant of the fact that many people are "by nature" homosexual and therefore should act according to their God-given homosexuality, is unacceptable to Orthodox Christian faith. No one in Orthodox Christian tradition has ever interpreted this text in this way, nor can anyone do so, according to Orthodoxy, when they read the Bible as a whole. On the contrary, the biblical teaching is rather this: The fact that many people have sexual feelings and desires for persons of their own sex is among the most powerful proofs that human being and life have been distorted by sin.

According to Orthodox Christian interpretation, the Bible also teaches that as time goes by, things will become more confused and difficult for humanity. In St. Luke's Gospel, Jesus even asks whether the Son of man will find faith on earth at His coming (Luke 18:8). In this view, as human nature and society become more darkened and disintegrated, the number of people with same-sex attractions and passions, and, indeed, with confused and deformed desires of all kinds, will dramatically increase and multiply. When contemplating this traditional Christian conviction, we cannot help but recall the fourth-century saying of St. Anthony the Great, who predicted, "A time is coming when [people] will go mad, and when they see someone who is not mad, they will attack [them] saying, 'You are mad, you are not like us.'" [10]

1 See Ps. 19 and Ps. 119; Amos 9:11–12; John 6:41–59.

2 Until our time, most Christians listened to God's Word; they did not read it for themselves. We also remember that God's Word is naturally written on human hearts.

On both these points, the witness of St. Anthony of Egypt is particularly pertinent. In both the "logia" attributed to him in *The Sayings of the Desert Fathers* (Ward, pp. 1–7), and in the seven letters attributed to him, he teaches that if people do not first follow God's "implanted Word" (compare James 1:21) in their nature and heart, they will not recognize God's Word incarnate "in words" in the Bible and "in person" as Jesus of Nazareth. See Samuel Rubenson, *The Letters of Anthony* (Minneapolis: Fortress Press, 1995). On the many evils caused by ignorance of Scripture, see St. John Chrysostom, *On Romans*, Homily 1 and *On Hebrews*, Homily 8.

3 A summary of this biblical and patristic teaching is found in *The Arena, An Offering to Contemporary Monasticism* by St. Ignatius Brianchaninoff (Jordanville, NY: Holy Trinity Monastery, 1997). See also *The Ladder of Divine Ascent* by St. John Climakos (Boston: Holy Transfiguration Monastery, 1991).

4 In the *Sayings of the Desert Fathers*, we find this among the words attributed to Poemen (called the Shepherd): "Abraham, the disciple of Abba Agathon, questioned Abba Poemen saying, 'How do the demons fight against me?' Abba Poemen said to him, 'The demons fight against you? They do not fight against us at all as long as we are doing our own will. For our own wills become the demons, and it is these which attack us in order that we may fulfill them. But if you want to see who the demons really fight against, it is against Moses and those who are like him'" (*Poemen*, 67). He also said, "When self-will and ease become habitual, they overthrow a man" (83). He also said, "The will of man is a brass wall between him and God, and a stone of stumbling. When a man renounces it, he is also saying to himself, 'By my God, I can leap over a wall' [Ps. 18:29]" (54). Also Dorotheos of Gaza, "I know of no other way in which a person can fall other than by trusting in his own heart. Some people say that a person falls for this or that reason. I, however, as I said, have never seen another kind of fall that is not caused by this. 'Have you seen somebody fall?' Know that he trusted himself. There is nothing more serious than to trust yourself, nothing is more pernicious." *Practical Teaching on the Christian Life*, Lesson 5, "That one should not trust his own understanding" (C. Scouteris, Translation, introduction and glossary, Athens, 2000), p. 127. In his version of *Unseen Warfare* (Crestwood, NY: SVS Press, 1978), St. Theophan the Recluse says that only total trust in God and complete mistrust of self, together with ceaseless prayer and constant striving, result in victorious living for humans in the fallen world.

5 The prayer of the Orthodox Divine Liturgy before the Gospel reading: "Illumine our hearts, O Master, with the light of Your divine knowledge. Open our minds to the understanding of the Gospel. Implant in us the fear of Your blessed commandments, that trampling down all carnal desires we may enter upon a spiritual manner of living, both thinking and doing such things as are well pleasing in Your sight. For You are the illumination of our souls and bodies, O Christ our God, and to You we give glory together with Your unoriginate Father and Your all-holy, good and life-creating Spirit, now and ever and unto ages of ages. Amen."

6 On the biblical texts that deal specifically with homosexuality, see Thomas E. Schmidt, *Straight and Narrow? Compassion and Clarity in the Homosexuality Debate*

(Downers Grove, IL: InterVarsity Press, 1995) and Robert Gagnon, *The Bible and Homosexual Practice: Texts and Hermeneutics* (Nashville, TN: Abingdon Press, 2001).

7 See Lev. 18—21. No evidence exists anywhere in the New Testament writings that homosexual acts can be considered an expression of godly love in Christ. There is also no reference anywhere in the Gospels and apostolic writings that suggests the Mosaic laws concerning human sexual behavior are of the same nature as laws about ritual impurity, circumcision, or foods. It is rather the case that sexual behavior is made stricter in the New Testament than it was in the Old, being a return to what was "from the beginning," that is, according to God's original intention and purpose for humanity.

8 Matt. 5:17–48; 19:3–12; 1 Cor. 6:9–20; Eph. 5; Col. 3, and others.

9 See all of Matt. 5:17–48, ending with the words, "Therefore you shall be perfect, just as your Father in heaven is perfect."

10 St. Anthony the Great, *The Sayings of the Desert Fathers*, Saying 25. See also Anthony 23, Ischyrion 1, and others. Also St. Ignatius Brianchaninoff's *The Arena*. Also in our time, *Abbot Nikon, Letters to Spiritual Children* (Richfield Springs, NY: Nikodemos Orthodox Publication Society, 1997).

—13 —

Same-Sex Attraction and Blessed Mourning

ORTHODOX CHRISTIAN SCRIPTURES AND SAINTS all stress the necessity, and indeed the inevitability, of blessed mourning (*penthos*) over life in this sinful world. They say, as is often emphasized in Orthodox Church services, that without tears of sorrow over the "sin of the world" and one's own sins, and those of one's family and friends, no person can be saved. A human being who sees and experiences the grim realities of life in this world will necessarily weep as Jesus wept, and weep together with Him. "Blessed are they who mourn," Christ teaches, "for they shall be comforted" (Matt. 5:4).

According to apostolic Christian teaching, there are two kinds of grief. There is worldly grief (*tou kosmou lype*), which produces death. This grief comes when people fail to get what they want according to their sinful and self-centered passions and desires. This grief intensifies when people are told they should fight their sinful passions by God's grace, rather than allow themselves to be enslaved by them. And then there is godly grief (*kata theon lype*), which produces a repentance that leads to life. This is the grief of blessed mourning over the consequences of sin in human being and life (2 Cor. 7:8–13).

Jesus shows godly grief, accompanied by godly anger, when He encounters human hardheartedness in the name of God and legalistic religion (see Mark 3:5, and others). St. Paul also displays such grief and anger when he agonizes over those who "have a zeal for

God" that is "not according to knowledge" (*ou kat'epignosin*), and who thereby replace God's righteousness with a righteousness of their own (Rom. 10:2–3).

"The sacrifices of God are a broken spirit, / A broken and a contrite heart— / These, O God, You will not despise" (Ps. 51:17). This line of the most repeated psalm in Orthodox Church worship is confirmed by Shadrach's prayer in the fiery furnace in Babylon, which is chanted, with the entire Canticle of the Three Young Men, over Christ's tomb at the Vesperal Divine Liturgy on the eve of Pascha.

> At this time we have become fewer than any nation, and are brought low in all the world because of our sins. At this time there is no prince, or prophet, or leader, no burnt offering, or sacrifice, or oblation, or incense, no place to make an offering before You or to find mercy. Yet with a contrite heart and a humble spirit may we be accepted. . . . Such may our sacrifice be in Your sight this day, and may we wholly follow You, for there will be no shame for those who trust in You. And now with all our heart we follow You, we fear You and seek Your face. Do not put us to shame, but deal with us in Your forbearance and in Your abundant mercy. Deliver us in accordance with Your marvelous works, and give glory to Your name, O Lord! Let all who do harm to Your servants be put to shame; let them be disgraced and deprived of all power and dominion, and let their strength be broken. Let them know that You are the Lord, the only God, glorious over the whole world. (Song of the Three Young Men 14–22)

This is the "prayer of prayers" of grieving sinners before the face of God. It is surely the prayer of Christians who blessedly mourn their sins, and the sins of the world, from which they have been redeemed and delivered by the crucified Christ. As such, it is the perfect prayer of those who weep over a wounded humanity enslaved to sinful sexual passions, heterosexual and homosexual.[1]

1 "When our soul leaves this world we shall not be blamed for not having worked miracles, or for not having been theologians, or not having been rapt in divine visions. But we shall certainly have to give an account to God of why we have not ceaselessly mourned." St. John Climakos, *The Ladder of Divine Ascent*, 7.70.

— 14 —

Same-Sex Attraction and Joy

IN ORTHODOX CHRISTIAN TRADITION, blessed mourning is always accompanied by ineffable joy.[1] For this reason, the saints call such grieving "joy-producing mourning" (*charopoion penthos*).[2] It is the joyful sadness that comes from enduring afflictions for the sake of truth and righteousness, and from grieving over the evils of the world in the light of God's mercy and love (Matt. 5:10–12). Thus the Apostle Paul writes that Christians not only rejoice in their hope of sharing the glory of God in Christ, but they also "rejoice in [their] sufferings," through which they "fill up . . . what is lacking in the afflictions of Christ, for the sake of His body, which is the church" (Col. 1:24).[3]

Therefore, having been justified by faith, we have peace with God through our Lord Jesus Christ, through whom also we have access by faith into this grace in which we stand, and rejoice in hope of the glory of God. And not only that, but we also glory in tribulations, knowing that tribulation produces perseverance; and perseverance, character; and character, hope. Now hope does not disappoint, because the love of God has been poured out in our hearts by the Holy Spirit who was given to us (Rom. 5:1–5).[4]

Christians who suffer afflictions because of their resistance to their sinful desires, their sorrows over the sinful actions that these passions have forced them to, and their agonies and pains from the scorn heaped on them by sinners with the insanity to "cast the stone" against them, will come to rejoice in all these afflictions, sorrows, agonies, and pains as their faith in Jesus grows and matures.[5] They will also come to know for themselves the truth of Christ's promise to His disciples before His Passion that "in the world you will have tribulation, but be of good cheer [take courage], I have overcome the world" (John 16:33).[6]

Sadly, many of us sinners, whatever our sexual attractions, never come to taste the joy and peace in the Holy Spirit that comes with suffering in and with Jesus, because we never fully surrender to the Lord and never completely succeed in ceasing to surrender to our sinful passions with blessed mourning. We live in some in-between state, being neither here nor there. As some saints have put it, we have left Egypt but have not entered the Promised Land; we dwell perpetually in the desert. And so we remain miserable and unhappy. We have not yet experienced the truth that we find divine happiness in "the blessed life" only when we take up our crosses without condition, and not merely (if at all) to the degree that we deem desirable and reasonable according to our own thinking and choosing.

1 St. John Chrysostom writes, "Now this joy is not contrary to that mourning; it is even born from it. He who weeps for his evil deeds [and the world's sin] and admits them is in joy. To put the same thing in another way; it is possible to be in mourning for one's own sins and in joy because of Christ." *On Philippians*, 14. See I. Hausherr, *Penthos: The Doctrine of Compunction in the Christian East* (Kalamazoo, MI: Cistercian Publications, 1982), p. 140. St. Seraphim of Sarov insisted that the purpose of human life is the "acquisition of the Holy Spirit," which he defined not only as the acquisition of God's virtues and characteristics (love, peace, joy, patience, wisdom, righteousness, etc.), but also as the ability to see one's wretchedness, and that of the whole world, and to remain peaceful and joyful because of God's grace and mercy. See V. Zander, *St. Seraphim of Sarov* (Crestwood, NY: SVS Press, 1975).

2 See St. John Climakos, *The Ladder of Divine Ascent*, Step 7.

3 I once asked my professor of theology, Serge S. Verhovskoy, what could possibly be lacking in Christ's sufferings and afflictions for the sake of our salvation. His answer was, "Our personal participation in them."

4 See also 1 Pet. 4:12–19.

5 The story of the woman caught in adultery found in some ancient versions of St.

John's Gospel (7:53—8:11) is essential to our topic. It is the paradigm for our dealing with sin in general, and sexual sin in particular.

6 Another translation of this sentence might be, "In the world you have affliction, but take courage, I have conquered the world." See 1 John 5:4–5; Rev. 2:7, 11, 17, 26; 3:5, 12, 21; 5:5; 6:2; 17:14; 21:7; and others.

— 15 —

Same-Sex Attraction and Friendship

LIKE PERSONS WITH HETEROSEXUAL DESIRES, persons with same-sex attractions who have an Orthodox Christian experience of reality will cultivate wholesome spiritual friendships with as many good and wise people as they can.[1] They will also cherish special relationships with a small number of men and women, some of whom will be their dearest elders and closest companions on the way of love in Christ. And they will additionally seek out therapeutic relationships, particularly with persons of their same sex, in order to deal with same-sex developmental issues that must be resolved for their emotional and spiritual healing.

People of predominantly or exclusively same-sex attractions and desires will know that they must work and pray to find and nourish deep, close, and lasting friendships with persons of their own sex with whom they have no erotic sexual relations. They will do so especially if they find some credence in the theory that among the causes of their same-sex feelings is some sort of traumatic break with their same-sex parent or adult caregiver in early childhood.[2] Whatever the causes of a person's sexual feelings and desires, however, it remains a firm conviction of Orthodox Christianity that healthy and holy people always have friends of both sexes with whom they learn to love in all the ways God commands human beings to love. Another firm conviction is that some of these special spiritual friends have to be older and wiser than they are.[3]

Christian history, beginning with the Bible, demonstrates

without exception that saints always come in clusters. Most of them have holy parents. All have spiritual fathers, mothers, sisters, and brothers with whom they share their lives and struggles in the most intimate and candid ways, on the deepest levels. They also have intense and intimate friendships with persons of both sexes.[4]

Christian history, beginning with the Bible, also demonstrates without exception that saints involved in godly friendships never engaged in erotic sexual activities or unions with persons to whom they were not married. Despite the intensity of their love for one another and the depth of their intimate bonding, there is not the remotest insinuation in the Bible or church history, for example, that Jonathan and David, Naomi and Ruth, Sergius and Bacchus, Basil the Great and Gregory the Theologian, or John Chrysostom and Olympia ever had sexual intercourse with each other in any form; not to speak of Jesus and His beloved disciple John, or Jesus and Lazarus, or Jesus and Mary Magdalene.[5]

1 See Paul D. O'Callaghan, *The Feast of Friendship* (Wichita, KS: Eighth Day Press, 2002). Fr. Paul is the pastor of St. George Orthodox Cathedral in Wichita, Kansas.

2 Elizabeth Moberly holds that homosexual emotions and desires are caused by a traumatic break in early childhood between the child and its parent (or main adult caregiver) of the same gender. She sees the failure of most psychological therapy with homosexual people as rooted in the failure to see this, and in wrongly thinking that the homosexual's problem is one of relating to the opposite sex. She holds firmly to the view that people with homosexual passions must counsel with therapists of their own gender with whom they can interrelate in love, in order to provide what was missing in the person's emotional and sexual development in childhood. She is convinced that the childhood trauma that causes homosexuality can often be identified, and that deep and lasting healing can occur with proper therapy, counseling, and prayer. She thinks that I can be more optimistic on this point than I am in these reflections. See E. Moberly, *Homosexuality: A New Christian Ethic* (Cambridge, England: James Clarke & Co and Greenwood, SC: The Attic Press, 1983). See also E. Moberly, *Psychogenesis: The Early Development of Gender Identity* (London, Boston, Melbourne: Routledge & Kegan Paul Ltd, 1964).

3 See the comments on friendship in St. Maximus the Confessor's *Fourth Century on Love*, 92–99.

4 Examples of holy families abound, beginning with Mary, Joseph, and Jesus; and Zacharias, Elizabeth, and John the Baptist. The Cappadocian families of Basil the Great, Gregory of Nyssa, and Gregory the Theologian are also exemplary. There are also a number of outstanding spiritual friendships, e.g. Basil and Gregory, Cassian and Germanus, Euthymios and Theoktistos, Sergius and Bacchus, Chrysostom and Olympia, Seraphim of Sarov and his nuns, Nektarios of Aegina and his nuns; and, in the West, Francis of Assisi and Clare, John of the Cross and Teresa, Francis of Sales and Jeanne de Chantal, and others.

5 The Bible makes no mention of sexual activity between David and Jonathan, but has much to say about David and Bathsheba. For the relationship between David and Jonathan, see St. John Chrysostom, *On First Corinthians*, Homily 33. In his funeral oration for Basil the Great, Gregory the Theologian said that they were "one soul in two bodies." This was also said about St. John Cassian and Germanus, and St. Euthymios the Great and Theoktistos. My professor of theology, Serge S. Verhovskoy, often claimed that the love between John Chrysostom and the widowed deaconess Olympia was the greatest example of Christian love in church history.

—16—

Same-Sex Attraction and Sexual Activity

PEOPLE WITH SAME-SEX ATTRACTIONS, like all people, necessarily incorporate their sexuality into all their relationships. There is no aspect of human being and life devoid of a sexual dimension. There are no human activities, including worship, contemplation, and prayer, without a sexual component. Human beings always are, and act as, men and women, whether they are homosexual or heterosexual, married or single, monastic or secular. This is so no matter how difficult, painful, and confusing the specifically sexual elements of their being and life may be; or how powerful their sexual passions; or how genuine their love for people of their own and the opposite sex.

Orthodox Christianity also contends that there are proper ways of sexual expression and action that apply to everyone without exception, heterosexual or homosexual. When these ways are betrayed, they do not bring God's wrathful censure and punishment in some direct, legalistic, vindictive, and punitive manner.[1] They are rather deviations that bring their own intrinsic "censure" and "punishment," which may indeed be experienced as quite "wrathful," because they are contrary to the reality of things as God made them to be. Diseases and afflictions resulting from sinful behavior may be taken as examples of this truth, as may emotional and mental pains and sufferings resulting from the absence of love. A critical point in the Genesis story is that the Lord did not tell Adam and Eve that if they ate of "the tree of the knowledge of good and evil" He would *kill* them. He rather told them that should they eat of this "tree," or, in Eve's version, even should they touch it, they would *die* (Gen. 2:17; 3:3).

As we noted above, Orthodox Christianity contends that sexual intercourse can only be what God willed it to be within an unconditionally committed, completely faithful, and everlastingly enduring marriage of complementary love between a man and a woman—a marriage that combines charity (*agape*), friendship (*philia*), affection (*storge*), and the desire for chaste and holy union (*eros*) in God's service. Such love never begins with sexual activity. Nor is it defined by it, sustained by it, or perfected by it in itself. The act of sexual union between a married man and woman is always rather the climactic completion of their mutual love for one another in spirit and truth, which is ultimately perfected in God. The sexual act is the act that reveals and seals the authenticity of their mutual faith and love in oneness of mind and heart, a oneness that is ever more perfectly fulfilled in the unending delight of communion with God through Christ and the Holy Spirit in the age to come. In this sense, godly conjugal union in this age is, paradoxically, a symbol and foretaste of humanity's conjugal union with God in the age to come, in which, as we have already noted, there will be no sexual intercourse between creatures of any kind.

In this perspective, the sexual communion of love in marriage is like the participation in Holy Communion at the Church's Divine Liturgy. The fulfillment of the total conjugal commitment enables sexual union to be, like a worthy participation in Christ's Body and Blood in the Holy Eucharist, "for the forgiveness of sins, the healing of soul and body, and everlasting life" for those who partake "in a worthy manner." And it is "unto condemnation and judgment" for those who partake unworthily.[2]

We must also note again that the point we are trying to make here applies equally, and even in the first instance, to sexual acts within heterosexual marriages that may be legally and ecclesiastically valid, but are devoid of the perfecting elements of divine love. This is especially true of marriages in which sexually active spouses do not intend to fulfill their "union of conjugal love" by bearing and caring for children in their ongoing life together, when they are perfectly capable of doing so.[3]

Another conviction universally held in Orthodox Christian tradition is that oral/genital and anal/genital acts of sexual intercourse, including those between married men and women, are a misuse and abuse of our bodies created to "glorify God" as "members of Christ" and "temples of the Holy Spirit," since each of our bodily members has its own holy use (1 Cor. 6:9–20; Rom. 12:1). In this view, such actions can hardly be expressions of divine love.

Another conviction in Orthodox Christian tradition is that masturbation is also a misuse and abuse of one's body. This is especially the case with married men and women, whose bodies are not their own, but belong to their spouses (1 Cor. 7:4).[4] It seems that obsessive masturbation (and not simply the experimentation with one's body that inevitably happens in growing up in this world) is caused by the pain, unhappiness, and loneliness that result from being the object of abusive behavior such as neglect, ridicule, threatening, frightening, beating, and sexual titillation and molestation. This obsession can also result from being sinfully pampered and catered to in unhealthy ways, without proper physical, emotional, and spiritual guidance and discipline. We must also acknowledge that the wholesale acceptance and encouragement of masturbation in our culture is a significant factor. Whatever its causes, however, masturbation is not an activity befitting people made for divine love in God's image and likeness. As the habit of masturbation grows, it becomes destructively compulsive and addictive, and it inhibits sexual loving as God wills it to be.

We may also observe at this point that an inevitable consequence of childhood abuse, whatever its forms, is an overwhelming tendency in the abused to self-centeredness and self-defensiveness. Those of us who have suffered great pain in childhood, especially from adults whom we should have been able to trust and live with in love and happiness, tend to receive any criticism of our behavior, no matter how just and helpful, as an attack, a punishment, and a beating. We even feel attacked, beaten, and punished when we hear God's commandments. The wrath is always for us, we feel, while the mercy is always for others. Going to church services can be extremely painful for us. At times it produces an almost unbearable anger and grief.[5] This is especially so when we observe the sins and failings of others, particularly our parents, elders, and those in any kind of authority over us, who deprive us of their love. I note this here because people with same-sex attractions and emotions are surely with the rest of us who have been so abused, and they share with us the anger, sadness, self-absorption, defensiveness, and aggression that we so often experience because of our wounds.

---

1 Some Christians believe that Christ's "payment of the price" on the cross is the payment of the debt of punishment that God must exact from sinners. I am convinced that according to the Orthodox understanding of Christian faith, the debt that Christ pays on the cross to ransom sinners from death is rather the debt of righteousness and love that God requires of His creatures, which humans have all failed to give. I believe that the Christian faith according to Orthodoxy does not hold that God punishes anyone for anything, though the Lord certainly does chastise sinners in their earthly lives so that they might repent of their sins before they stand judgment before Christ at His coming. At the Lord's parousia, we may also note, every person is judged by God's divine mercy, which is given to all people in Jesus. The "punishment" of Gehenna, therefore, is a punishment that unrepentant sinners inflict upon themselves when they suffer torment "from the face [or presence] of the Lord," who loves and forgives them. We note here as well that the words "exclusion from" in the English RSV translation of 2 Thess. 1:9 do not exist in the original Greek text.

2 Marriage in the Orthodox sacramental rite appears as a kind of "baptism" of the couple, who have already each been personally baptized into Christ and sealed by the Holy Spirit. The man and woman to be married are met at the entrance of the church, where they make their pledges to each other and put on rings. They are then led into the center of the assembly where, after lengthy prayers abounding in biblical allusions for God to "join together what has been rent asunder," crowns are placed on (or over) their heads with the singing of Psalm 8:5 and 21:3–4. They then hear the epistle (Eph. 5:21–

33) and Gospel (John 2:1–11), join in saying (or singing) the Lord's Prayer, drink together from a common cup (originally Holy Communion), and process three times around a holy table (originally, most likely, the altar table itself) following the Cross held high in the hands of the bishop or priest. Therefore, to continue the analogy, just as unbaptized (or baptized) persons who are not wholly committed to Christ in faith and love may not partake of Holy Communion, and if they do, their action would be "unto condemnation and judgment"; so unmarried (or married) men and women who are not wholly committed to each other in faith and love may not have sexual intercourse with each other, and if they do, they bring condemnation and judgment upon themselves for defiling what is holy.

3 We are not referring here to couples who may know that they will not have children for reasons beyond their will or control. We have in mind only those who are fully capable of having children but intentionally decide not to do so for sinful, selfish reasons.

4 The entire seventh chapter of 1 Corinthians, about the mutual belonging and submission of husband and wife—like Ephesians 5:21–33, which was so radical for the early Church—is crucial for our topic. We may note here as well that an interpretation of this chapter that would claim the apostle teaches that celibacy is "higher" than marriage for theological and mystical reasons may be incorrect. It seems rather that he is giving the pragmatic advice that if a person is radically committed to Christ and the Gospel, especially in a time of severe persecution and suffering, when "the end" is at hand, it is on a practical level much easier to be single than to be married.

5 Some spiritual writers allegorize the biblical "fire" and "water" that God's faithful people must be led through in order to reach the "spacious place." The fire is the *anger* that they feel over their sins, and those of others; and the water is the *tears* that they shed in godly grief and blessed mourning. The "spacious place" is dispassionate peace and love. For example, see Psalm 66.

— 17 —

Same-Sex Attraction and Sexual Knowing

IN THE BIBLE, THE VERB "TO KNOW" IS USED for sexual intercourse. When a couple "know" each other in an act of sexual union, they are joined in a psychospiritual connection that forever affects their being and life in the most basic and radical ways. St. Paul even claims that those who join themselves to prostitutes become "one body" with them in ways that have consequences that can never be reversed or erased—though they can be forgiven and healed, as is true of all the acts of our earthly existence (1 Cor. 6:16).

Godly sexual "knowing," therefore, can occur only when married men and women enact sexual intercourse in the loving manner designed by God. All other kinds of sexual "knowing" are contrary to godly life and divine love. They cannot be the "knowing" that God intends for His people in sexual union. Such "knowing," be it heterosexual or homosexual, will necessarily lead to dissatisfaction, unhappiness, and death, both spiritual and physical. It is simply not life-creating and life-enhancing. And the "god" known in such "knowing" is always an idol, the product of creaturely imagination and fantasy.

The knowledge of "the only true God and Jesus Christ whom He has sent," which, according to St. John's Gospel, is "eternal life" (John 17:3), is never attained in "sexual knowing" outside marriage. Knowledge of God comes only in being known and loved by God, and in imitating and participating in God's knowledge and love for us. We can imitate and participate in this divine knowledge and love, desiring it with all our hearts, even in our sexual actions.[1] The apostolic principle that in perfect love we come to know fully, "face to face" (*prosopon pros prosopon*), and not merely "in part" (*ek merous*), and that in perfect love we come to know fully even as we are fully known, applies perfectly to sexual love (see 1 Cor. 13:12). Such face-to-face knowing and being fully known in perfect love, we affirm once more, according to the Christian experience of things, happens sexually only in fully committed conjugal love between a man and a woman.

---

1 See Gal. 4:8–9; 1 Cor. 13:12; 1 John 4:7–12. The evangelical rule that "with the same measure that you use, it will be measured back to you," which "good measure" will be "pressed down, shaken together, and running over" (Luke 6:38), applies also to sexual giving. In the Orthodox Christian view, such sexual giving can only be accomplished in committed marriages between men and women.

— 18 —

Same-Sex Attraction and Children

MEN AND WOMEN WITH SAME-SEX ATTRACTIONS and desires may certainly care for children with love and affection. They may visit and adopt orphans and other children abandoned by their families or unable to be cared for by them. They may take these children into their homes in order to raise them in divine love in a family setting. In doing this good work, they fulfill the apostolic definition of "pure and undefiled religion before God and the Father," which is "to visit orphans and widows in their trouble, and to keep oneself unspotted from the world" (James 1:27).

According to Orthodoxy, however, only those striving to keep themselves "unspotted from the world" may be blessed and approved to care for children. Unmarried people engaging in sexual intercourse with each other, not to speak of multiple partners, should not be permitted to adopt or care for children. And people of the same sex who are caring for children in their homes may not present themselves as the children's "parents," whatever the nature and character of their sexual relations with each other.

Since Orthodox Christian faith requires that children be the product of the godly love of their parents, pregnancies in any way involving anyone other than the potential child's biological father and mother are considered to be contrary to God's will, and so to divine love. In this view, gay men may not arrange for women to bear children for them. And lesbians may not arrange to become pregnant from the sperm of known or anonymous donors, whatever the means of their impregnation. Orthodox Christians are never-theless bound to love those engaging in these ways of procreating and caring for children, and surely the children themselves, with the same love and care that they owe all people in Christ and the Holy Spirit. And Orthodox pastors and church workers are to serve them, in word and deed, with every evangelical and philanthropic act of mercy they can possibly provide.

— 19 —

Same-Sex Attraction and Civil Rights

WHETHER OR NOT MEN AND WOMEN with same-sex attractions are struggling to resist engaging in erotic sexual activity, their civil rights, and the rights of the children in their care, must be guaranteed and safeguarded. Homosexual people must have the same access to housing, employment, police protection, legal justice, tax benefits, and visitation privileges at institutions that all members of society possess and enjoy. Those desiring to be joined in "civil unions" or "domestic partnerships" for such purposes should be allowed to do so, with the social and legal benefits that are guaranteed by such arrangements. This is especially important today, when the safety of homosexual people and their children largely depends on legal and social recognition and protection. It is also important because those in same-sex relationships, whether or not they are sexually active, almost always understand a denial of such public recognition and protection as an expression of hatred and contempt toward themselves and their families.[1]

I firmly believe that God commands His people to affirm and defend the civil rights and benefits of those who believe and do things that are contrary to His will (Luke 6:27–38; Rom. 12:14–21). Orthodox Scriptures and saints unanimously witness that justice and charity are to be extended to all human beings, without condition or discrimination. Even when a recalcitrant brother or sister in the believing community "refuses even to hear the church" and so by Christ's command is to be treated "like a heathen and a

83

tax collector," such a person is still to be fed when hungry, given drink when thirsty, clothed when naked, sheltered when homeless, and visited when sick or imprisoned (Matt. 18:15–20; 25:31–46). Such people are also to be treated justly in every way and to be afforded all protections and benefits of society. That they are not admitted to the Holy Eucharist does not mean that they are to be hated, scorned, or dealt with unjustly or uncharitably in any way. The apostolic rule for Christians is clear: "Do not be overcome by evil, but overcome evil with good" (Rom. 12:21). This corresponds to Christ's prayer before His Passion that God His Father should not take His disciples out of the world, but that He should keep them from the evil one (John 17:15).

Christians have no right to proclaim God's Gospel in Jesus to anyone whom they do not love in deeds as well as in words (1 John 3:18). They have no right to teach, and still less to prophesy to, those whom they do not respect and honor as being made in God's image, and whom they do not see as being saved together with them in the world so loved by God for which Christ has given His life. The Christian's highest calling is to advocate with Christ, His holy Mother, and all the saints, before the Face of God "on behalf of all and for all."[2] The Christian's noblest work is to intercede with the Lord, always and everywhere, for everyone and everything. We Orthodox actualize this divine calling every time we celebrate the Divine Liturgy. We cannot do it with impunity if we are at the same time denying basic human and civil rights to anyone, especially to those who may hold us and our convictions in greatest contempt and derision.

While upholding the civil and legal rights of everyone without discrimination, those professing Orthodox Christianity may never bless or countenance unions between persons of the same sex that contend to be *marriages* in the same sense as marriages between men and women. Where such unions are called "marriages" by civil law, Orthodox Christians are obliged to tolerate them as they tolerate, for example, laws allowing divorce, remarriage, and abortion, but they cannot approve or affirm them as acceptable to human being and life. Such "marriages" can only be understood, once again, as social and legal arrangements for practical purposes that are, in fact, the product of people who have largely lost the basic intuitions concerning human being and behavior that Christians believe are implanted in human hearts, witnessed to in the Bible, and actualized in Jesus Christ.[3]

Words, of course, important as they are, are still relative. Some Orthodox Christians may therefore reasonably argue that engaging in a bitter legal battle over the word "marriage" is unreasonable and counterproductive. This may be so first of all because most marriages between men and women, including those who call themselves Christians, and even Orthodox Christians, are so far from what they should be that they are hardly recognizable as Christian; and secondly because in our present setting opposition to the word "marriage" for gay people will almost always be construed (as we noted above) as expressing hatred and contempt.

Be that as it may, it remains an Orthodox Christian conviction that marriage was intended from the beginning to be a union between one man and one woman for the purpose of becoming "one flesh" in God. It exists for expressing human wholeness, and so for allowing humanity (*anthropos*) to be truly human, through an integration of the sexes in divine love. It also exists for procreating children, founding families, saving souls, serving neighbors (including enemies), and sanctifying the world. And before and above all else, it exists to glorify God, the Creator, Redeemer, and Sanctifier of all things in Christ and the Holy Spirit.

We may note at this point that the Orthodox Church's rite for "brother-making" or "sister-making" (or "brother-sister-making"), called in Greek *adelphopoiesis*, which some promoters of homosexual unions consider to be a service of "same-sex marriage," has nothing whatsoever to do with either homosexuality or marriage. It is a church service used when people of the same or opposite sexes wish to be formally and publicly bound in a relation of kinship for spiritual, and in some cases, legal or practical purposes. This service is rarely practiced today, but it still occurs on occasion in some Orthodox churches. People in such relationships are certainly not married to each other, though they may be married to others. And they are hardly permitted by this rite to engage in any kind of erotic sexual relations with each other.[4]

1 This point is powerfully and poignantly demonstrated in Sharon Underwood's op-ed piece in the *Valley News* of Lebanon, NH, during the time of the controversy over "civil unions" and "gay marriage" in Vermont. Those concerned with homosexuality must listen carefully to what this mother of a gay son, and others with her, including Congressman Bill Lippert of Vermont, have to say to them. Sharon Underwood's letter, with Congressman Lippert's testimony, are given in David Moat, *Civil Wars: A Battle for Gay Marriage* (Harcourt, 2004), pp. 213–218, 252–253.

2 The sacrificial gifts of bread and wine that become the Body and Blood of Christ are offered to God at the eucharistic liturgies of St. John Chrysostom and St. Basil the Great with the words "on behalf of all and for all [*kata panta kai dia panta*]."

3 See once again C. S. Lewis, *The Abolition of Man*.

4 See Peter Drobac, *Christian Friendship and Adelphopoiesis*, unpublished Master of Divinity thesis (St. Vladimir's Orthodox Theological Seminary, Crestwood, NY, 2004). Also Robin Darling Young, "Gay Marriage: Reimagining Church History," *First Things* 47 (1994): 43–48.

— 20 —

Same-Sex Attraction and Death

THE HIV/AIDS PANDEMIC OF OUR TIME has caused the death of millions of men, women, and children, a great many of whom were infected by the disease because of sexual activity, both homosexual and heterosexual. Some Christian (and non-Christian) interpreters take the pandemic as a prime example of the conviction that those who "eat of the tree of the knowledge of good and evil" bring death upon themselves for violating the laws of God and nature. Whatever the interpretation, the fact that HIV/AIDS is so closely connected with sexual activity, especially oral and anal intercourse between gay men, demands that a Christian theological interpretation of same-sex attraction and love concern itself directly with this fact.

Some exponents and critics of the gay and lesbian theologies that have emerged in recent decades, including the new so-called "queer" theologies, have blamed these theologies for failing to confront and interpret the phenomenon of HIV/AIDS, as well as the phenomenon of violence against homosexuals, with sufficient attention and depth. Some have also claimed that when gay and lesbian thinkers deal with death, their treatment of this ultimate human issue has often proved superficial, unconvincing, and unhelpful to the real lives of real people.[1]

In whatever ways Orthodox Christians may interpret the scourge of HIV/AIDS and the acts of violence committed against gay men and lesbians, many by people claiming to be Christians, they are

87

certainly obliged to add this deadly disease, together with the crimes against homosexuals, to the long list of death-dealing evils of our time. They must confront these terrible realities with much greater attention, courage, and honesty than they have done to date.[2] To fail in this task would be especially reprehensible for those who claim Christ's resurrection from the dead and His victory over injustice and suffering to be their dominant conviction and the sole motivation for all their actions.

According to Orthodoxy, human beings were created with the potentiality to keep themselves alive forever. They failed to fulfill this potentiality when they broke communion with God, the source of their life and well-being. In their rebellion against God, humans lost their dominion over nature and became subject to its death-dealing powers. In this view, even the so-called "acts of God" or "acts of nature," like hurricanes and floods and tidal waves that bring massive destruction and death to human beings, are ultimately the responsibility of humans, who have failed in their governance of nature and proper direction of its forces. Thus, in a word, every human failure to control, manage, and use nature in the right way—not to speak of direct human violations, corruptions, and destructions of nature—leads inexorably to human suffering and death.

In this view of things, in which God Himself is always directly involved with His terrible yet always merciful pedagogy, humanity and nature are in need of redemption and salvation. There is no natural immortality of souls. There is no spiritual realm into which one enters through death, no matter how just and loving one may be. Death is never good in itself. It is always the enemy to be destroyed. It is, indeed, as St. Paul says, the very "last enemy" to be overcome (1 Cor. 15:26). Love may well be "as strong as death," as the Scriptures declare (Song 8:6), but human love is always in need of purification, salvation, and redemption by the God who is Love for it to be completely victorious over death, and so to be eternal.

Thus, in the Orthodox Christian perspective, the only answer to death is Jesus Christ, the new, real, and final Adam. He alone controls all the destructive and demonic forces in creation and conquers death. He alone rules over nature, relates to it properly, uses it rightly, directs its powers positively, and deifies it totally. He does this, paradoxically, by dying on the cross in perfect love for God His Father and His fellow human beings. He does this in order to transform the "wages of sin" that "is death" into the way of salvation that is eternal life (Rom. 6:20–23). This is the Christian faith that Orthodox believers see as the only way toward an understanding of death, especially with its many tragic aspects in relation to same-sex attraction, and sexuality generally.

1 See Elizabeth Stuart, *Gay and Lesbian Theologies*, pp. 65–77.

2 I believe that the issue of death and dying is in need of serious attention in contemporary Orthodoxy, especially in the West, where most members of the Church seem to be "pagans" before people die and "Platonists" afterwards. By this I mean that they beg the Church to keep people alive, healthy, and happy as long as possible, and then demand that the Church assure them after people die that their immortal souls are "in a better place, basking in heavenly bliss" no matter what they may have done in their earthly lives.

— 21 —

Same-Sex Attraction and Theology

Anthropological issues, particularly concerning gender and sexuality, are central theological themes in our postmodern times, especially for Christians. Whether they speak and write about God, Jesus, the Bible, liturgy, ethics, or spirituality, virtually all contemporary Christian thinkers and authors concern themselves with these issues, which, in my view, are for contemporary Christians what the disputes with gnosticism were for the first followers of Jesus, and what the many controversies over Jesus' person, nature, will, and activity were for Christians of later centuries.[1]

The task of Orthodox theology is to explain and elaborate the Christian "canon of faith" testified to in the canonical biblical Scriptures, particularly the New Testament writings that interpret the Old Testament in the light of Christ. Theology requires an accurate exegesis of the Bible, whose continuing explication and application constitutes the Church's holy Tradition (with a capital "T"). The formal testimonies to the Church's "rule of faith" are the liturgy with its prayers, hymns, icons, and rituals; the definitions and canons of the church councils that have been universally approved and accepted in Orthodoxy; and the witness of the Church's canonized saints, not for everything they said and did, but for the reasons that their lives and teachings are affirmed and glorified.

Orthodoxy holds that the theoretical vision of Christian faith is essentially connected to its existential experience in people's lives. Orthodoxy, therefore, is not against human experience, including sexual experience, as some allege. Exactly the opposite is true. Christian experience gives rise to the theological vision testified to in Scripture and Tradition. And the theological vision of the Bible and Tradition, in turn, informs and shapes the experience of which it is itself an essential element.

In Orthodox Christianity, vision (*theoreia*) and experience (*praxis*) are organically united and interconnected. They may be abstractly distinguished, but they cannot be existentially separated. The conviction that human vision and experience have been distorted and corrupted by sin, and, as such, require divine purification and restoration, is, as we have constantly repeated here, an essential part of the vision and experience of Christianity as understood, taught, and lived in the Orthodox Church. Because this is so, Orthodox believers have always been, and must always be, both radically respectful of human experience and radically suspicious of it. They are obliged to observe human experiences carefully and to assess them honestly. They accomplish this delicate task in the light of their sacramental and spiritual experience in the believing community.

Because of people's propensity to self-interest and delusion, especially in humanity's present condition, Christians submit their experiences, including their sexual experiences, to the experience of the Church as a whole, beginning with the experience of the Lord Jesus Christ as recorded in the Gospels, and that of His apostles, martyrs, and saints through history. Christians do not follow their own minds, hearts, and bodies. They remain, on the contrary, ever ready to change their minds, purify their hearts, and discipline their bodies, which are "members of Christ," as they strive to acquire "the mind of Christ" and "the Spirit of God" (1 Cor. 2:9–16; 6:15–20).[2]

When it comes to science, the same principle holds. For Orthodox Christianity, there is no truth—scientific or poetic, physical or metaphysical, literal or spiritual—that is contrary to Christian truth.

In fact, for Orthodoxy, there is no such thing as "Christian truth" as distinct from any other kind of truth. Truth is truth; it is the same for everyone. In this perspective, divine revelation is not only about God; it is about everything else as well. And created things also are all about the God who made them, and so, in that sense, are revelatory of God in His divine energies and operations in the world. This conviction permits us to apply the Council of Chalcedon's definition concerning divinity and humanity in Jesus to our theological knowledge and our knowledge of created things. We can say that theology and science are joined in an inseparable and indivisible union in which they are not mixed or fused together, nor are they changed in what they are and do in themselves.[3]

While taking the results of scientific study most seriously, Orthodox Christianity traditionally gives at least two warnings about science that are pertinent to the issue of same-sex attraction and love. The first is that natural science in itself is restricted to physical nature and human behavior. It is not concerned with metaphysical, spiritual, and divine things. It analyses, describes, and explains the manifold activities of physical and living things, including human beings with their unique characteristics and properties, but it says nothing about the origin, meaning, and destiny of that which it studies.

The second warning is that science is concerned with physical, animal, and human natures in their presently deformed forms, not in the forms in which God originally created them, nor in the state in which they will be in God's coming kingdom. Therefore, for example, the fact that a certain percentage of human beings is proven to be of "homosexual orientation" is irrelevant in a theological and moral discussion of same-sex attraction and love. It says nothing about human being and life according to God and Christ. It says nothing about what was intended for humanity from the beginning and will be for humanity at the end, in the resurrection of the dead beyond the boundaries of this world. It merely provides data (always welcome, interesting, tentative, and debatable) about sinful humanity in a disordered and corrupted world in need of salvation.

An additional warning that must also be noted today in respect to scientific findings is that political correctness and vested interests often make it immensely difficult for scientific opinions that do not conform to current conventions to get a fair and objective hearing.

1 The Orthodox convictions on these issues, of course, are that Jesus Christ is God's divine Son and Word with the very same divinity as the one God and Father, and that He is also a real human being with the very same humanity that all human beings have. Thus Jesus is confessed to be one person with two natures, wills, and operations: human and divine.

2 See also St. Seraphim of Sarov, "Conversation with Nicholas Motovilov," *Treasury of Russian Spirituality*, George Fedotov, ed. (London: Sheed and Ward, 1952), pp. 265–279.

3 The Chalcedonian formula uses four negative adverbs to characterize the union of divinity and humanity in Jesus. The "two natures" of Christ are said to be perfectly united in the Lord's one person (*prosopon* or *hypostasis*) in a union "without separation" (*adaiaretos*) and "without division" (*achoristos*), and also "without fusion" (*asyngetos*) and "without change" (*atreptos*).

— 22 —

Same-Sex Attraction and Religion

IN THE ORTHODOX VIEW, CHRISTIAN FAITH is not a "religion" (except in the conventional everyday use of the word). It is the fulfillment of all religions in their search for divine truth and human meaning as inspired by God's law written on human hearts. In this understanding, God's Gospel in Jesus is the end of all religions as human constructions, however good and inevitable they are in their desire to deal with life's mysteries and to comprehend the ways of God (or the gods) and creatures in a demon-riddled, death-bound world.

Christian faith and life, as witnessed in apostolic Scripture and the lives and teachings of the saints, belongs to a "new creation" (Gal. 6:15; 2 Cor. 6:17). It does not belong to "this age" whose "form is passing away"(1 Cor. 7:31).[1] It is "from above" and leads always to what is "beyond." It is not from human beings, and it transcends human history. It is not contrary to nature and reason, but surpasses their limitations. It discloses the original nature and purposes of things, reveals their ultimate destiny, and illumines human minds and hearts to "the knowledge of the truth" about God and all things in Him.[2] As such, Christian faith and life is God's gift of divine truth, light, wisdom, and power given to creatures as completely and perfectly as is now possible within the conditions of the corrupted cosmos.

When Christians understand Christ's Gospel to be but one of humankind's many religions, even the first, best, and greatest, the Gospel ceases to be what it is. It becomes but another product of sinful humanity in its fallen form: good, true, and beautiful in many ways, yet incomplete and dangerously deceptive. As such, it is inevitably deformed into an ideological mythology, or mythological ideology, employed to promote and defend the "merely human" and, inevitably, sinful persons and societies that use it for this deplorable purpose. This is so whether this Christian religion is fundamentalist and sectarian, or whether it is relativistic and inclusive, seeing itself as no better or worse, and essentially even no different from any other.

Those who consider their Christianity as a religion, whether sectarian or relativistic, inevitably see themselves as somehow superior to others who do not see things as they do. They are convinced that they possess a special calling to convince others of the truth they possess, whether they think they have this truth as a free gift or have discovered it for themselves by their diligent labors. And they understand themselves as called to save all others from the evils from which they themselves are free.

Such Christians do not see themselves as one with the "others" to whom they are sent. They do not present themselves as bound together with them in a common web of ignorance and enslavement from which only God can deliver them. They do not see themselves as God's sinful and unworthy servants, called to witness to the truth that God alone is the Savior and Lord "of all men [all people], especially of those who believe" (1 Tim. 4:10). And they refuse to confess that "Christ Jesus came into the world to save sinners, of whom [they themselves are] chief" (1 Tim. 1:12–17).

In a word, such persons and societies do not see themselves as those most in need, before all others, of the saving Gospel they proclaim and defend. And they do not identify themselves as the premier debtors to this divine truth, about which they personally have nothing to boast, before they would even think of proclaiming it to others. They do not allow themselves even to consider that they may, in fact, be mistaken about one or another, or even all, of their convictions. As such, they are never in dialogue. They never listen. They never converse. They are never at peace in themselves or with others. They are always in a crusade and a war that they must win at all costs. And it is exactly *they*, and not God, who must win it.

Examples abound of persons, communities, and societies that identify themselves as those empowered by God to lord it over others because of their special election. The foremost example of this for readers of the Bible is God's people Israel, whom the Lord irrevocably chose to be His servants for the salvation of the nations, but who took the calling for themselves in an erroneous and ungodly manner. Christian history is filled with such persons and groups. Orthodox Christians need only think of the mythologies and ideologies of Byzantium and Russia, within which the Church's saints, the real servants of the true God, were always rejected and persecuted.

Western Christians, with their peculiar understandings of predestination and election, can name their own particular version of this tragic error. American Christians can think of the USA, whose citizens have too often considered themselves as God's chosen people, with the divine mandate and manifest destiny to submit all others on earth to the right and true way of life for all people, which is, of course, the American Way. In the United States, we may also recall the rhetoric about the black people whom God raised up at the time of the civil rights movement of the 1960s to teach everyone how to be just, compassionate, peaceful, and loving. More recently, we see some Western and Western-educated women claiming such a special election for themselves, and for women generally. And still more recently, some gay men and lesbians have taken up this claim for themselves, with some of their bisexual and transgendered colleagues.

Orthodox Christians, if they be truly Christian and Orthodox, resist every temptation to identify themselves as anything other than an assembly of sinners without competence or calling to judge anyone for anything (Matt. 7:1–5).[3] They see themselves in no other way than as witnesses testifying to what, through no merit of their own, they have seen and heard and apply first of all to themselves.[4] They understand themselves solely as "servant[s] of all" in and with Jesus, so that "by all means" some, especially "the weak," may be saved with them (1 Cor. 9:19–23).[5] They "pommel" and "subdue" their own bodies, lest when they "have preached to others" they themselves "should become disqualified" (1 Cor. 9:27). They are eager even to be "accursed" and cut off from Christ so that their brothers and sisters might be saved and come to "the knowledge of the truth" that God wills for all people in the enjoyment of everlasting life (Rom. 9:3; 1 Tim. 2:4).[6] They, before all others, are terrified of being guilty of "casting the stone" at anyone for anything (John 8:7).

And, as paradoxical as it may seem, though it is perfectly appropriate to their faith, they live in the constant awareness that they may be mistaken in their most heartfelt convictions. Because of this, they never cease praying for the Holy Spirit to guide them into all truth and to bring to remembrance, purely and accurately, what Christ has revealed and declared to them, and to the whole world, of God (John 16:12–15). They know that no one is infallible. Thus they are ever ready to listen, to be corrected, and to repent when repentance is necessary.

For Orthodox Christians to fail to see themselves as sinners who exist solely as slaves for the healing and salvation of all people, with whom they are identified in every way, is egregiously reprehensible. It amounts to a betrayal of the very faith they claim to proclaim. It may even be a form of "blasphemy against the Holy Spirit," the "eternal sin" that "will not be forgiven, either in this age, or in the age to come" (Mark 3:28–29; Matt. 12:31–32; Luke 12:10).

---

1 English translations of the Bible sometimes use the word "world" for what in the original is "age." This is also done in translations of the Creed, where Christians confess

their expectation of "the life of the age [not world] to come." There is no world but this one; but there is a new "age" for this world. Also, according to Orthodoxy, the "new heaven and new earth" that we await is this earth and heaven made new, just as the "new creation" is the renewal and re-creation of the present good world, which has been corrupted. The Scripture does not say that God makes all new things; it rather says that God makes all things new. See Rev. 21:1–5. Also, Is. 65:17; 66:22. Also, I use the singular "it" for Christian faith and life, seeing these as one thing.

2 See 1 Tim. 2:4; 2 Tim. 3:7; Heb. 10:26. "Knowledge of truth [*epignosis aletheias*]" (with or without definite articles) is a technical scriptural expression often used in Orthodox liturgical prayers. For example, see the prayer of the First Antiphon and the first prayer of the Eucharistic Canon of the Divine Liturgy of St. Basil the Great.

3 "A demonic boy came one day to be healed, and some brothers from an Egyptian monastery arrived. As one old man was coming out to meet them he saw a brother sinning with the boy, but did not accuse him; he said 'If God who made them sees them and does not burn them, who am I to blame them?'" *The Sayings of the Desert Fathers*, John the Persian, 1. See also Isaac the Theban, 1, and others.

4 Gal. 1:6–17; Eph. 2:1–10; 1 John 1–4; and others.

5 1 Cor. 9:19–23 is the epistle reading at the Orthodox Divine Liturgy on the eve of Theophany.

6 St. Silouan the Athonite (d. 1938) said that "there is no greater miracle than to love the sinner in his fall," adding that "if you see a [person] sin and have no pity for him, grace will forsake you." He also repeatedly said that the sole proof of one's knowledge and love of God is unconditional love for one's enemies. See Archimandrite Sophrony (Sakharov), *St. Silouan the Athonite* (Essex, England: Stavropegic Monastery of St. John the Baptist and Crestwood, NY: SVS Press, 1991), pp. 346, 348, and throughout. Orthodox spiritual writers unanimously teach that God sees to it that people are soon tempted by the very sins they condemn others for committing.

— 23 —

Same-Sex Attraction and Church Community

ACCORDING TO ORTHODOX CHRISTIAN FAITH, Christ's one, holy, catholic, and apostolic Church is a concrete historical community of baptized believers governed by bishops in apostolic succession who teach apostolic doctrine, conduct apostolic worship, and preserve apostolic tradition. The bishops are consecrated with the ministry to "guard what was committed to [their] trust" and to "rightly divide the word of truth" (1 Tim. 6:20: 2 Tim. 1:12–14; 2:15). Each local community of believers headed by its bishop or priest is the one, holy Church of Christ in its catholic fullness. It is the ark of salvation for sinners, among whom each member, beginning with the bishop and priest, confesses him- or herself as "chief" (1 Tim. 1:15).[1] In this view, no bishop or see is infallible, and there is no infallible magisterium to be obeyed without question. Christ's Church lives by the presence and action of God, which always acts through human means without violating human freedom. The Church lives and acts by God's divine grace and power, which are neither magical nor mechanical.

Christ's Church is for all people who believe the Gospel and confess the Christian faith as they strive to repent of their sins and to resist their sinful passions, by which they expect to be tempted to their last breath.[2] For this reason, the local parish church will never be a wholly safe place for sinners to deal openly with their temptations and sins, since it is always comprised of sinners (including its pastors and leaders) at all stages of spiritual growth and

101

development. But groups can be found within the churches in which struggling Christians with sufficient spiritual maturity, including those with same-sex attractions and desires, can "come out" to others about the realities of their lives, including the sexual realities, without apprehension or fear.[3] We see this now happening where courageous believers connect with one another under the guidance of experienced elders in order to "bear one another's burdens, and so fulfill the law of Christ" (Gal. 6:2).

Although some extraordinary men and women have attained marvelous degrees of sanctity in this life, total spiritual healing for human beings is rarely, if ever, completed on earth. This is even more the case in regard to physical, psychological, and emotional healing, though some people have attained remarkable measures of healing before their deaths. We should never be discouraged or surprised about what God can accomplish in those willing to pay the price for life. But still, it is sadly true that healing in this world, according to Orthodox Christianity, is often restricted to our willingness and ability to discern and acknowledge evils and diseases, to claim them as our own, to suffer them with patience, to struggle with them with courage, and to forgive those who have caused and contributed to their effects in our lives, as we work to attain perfect wholeness and holiness only in the age to come.[4]

1 See the final prayer before Holy Communion in the Orthodox Prayer Book, which is recited corporately in some churches at the Divine Liturgy. Also T. Hopko, "The Orthodox Parish in North America," in *Speaking the Truth in Love* (Crestwood, NY: SVS Press, 2004), pp. 85–95.

2 "Abba Anthony said to Abba Poemen, 'This is the great work of a man: always to take the blame [responsibility] for his own sins before God and to expect temptation [trial, testing] to his last breath.' He also said, 'Whoever has not experienced temptation cannot enter the kingdom of Heaven.' He even added, 'Without temptations no one can be saved.'" Ward, *The Sayings of the Desert Fathers*, Anthony the Great, 4, 5, p. 2. See also Theodora, 2, p. 71, and Syncletica, 25, p 197. (The sayings of three women are in the alphabetical list: Theodora, Syncletica, and Sarah.)

3 Gay and lesbian theologies routinely speak of "coming out" about one's sexuality as an "exodus" experience, which it is. (See Stuart, *Gay and Lesbian Theologies*.) Orthodox teachers see "exodus" as a liberation from "slavery" that does not immediately result in blissful life in "the promised land." It is always rather an exodus into the waterless and foodless "desert" filled with all kinds of enemies and demons, where the Lord's liberated people worship Him alone, receive His commandments, and do battle with His enemies by His power (Ex. 14:14). For Orthodox Christians, the "exodus experience" is never something social, political, national, or cultural. It is always a liberation from evil, sin, and death through the "exodus" that Christ "was to accomplish at Jerusalem," which He discussed with Moses and Elijah on the mountain of His transfiguration (Luke 9:31). It is the "pascha" and "exodus" of Christ's death and resurrection into God's glory.

4 St. John Chrysostom says somewhere that a person who is healed in this age from whatever malady and disease is always healed for "more crosses." The common teaching of the saints is that healings on earth are to give glory to God, confirm the faithful, convict the faithless, produce repentance, and/or allow more time to those who are healed to proclaim the Gospel, witness to Christ, struggle against sin, serve their neighbor, and fulfill their duties. The fathers sometimes say amazing things in this regard. "Abba Poemen said of Abba John the Dwarf that he had prayed to God to take his passions away from him so that he might be free from care. He went and told an old man this: 'I find myself in peace, without an enemy,' he said. The old man said to him, 'Go, beseech God to stir up warfare so that you may regain the affliction and humility that you used to have, for it is by warfare that the soul makes progress.' So he besought God and when the warfare came, he no longer prayed that it might be taken away, but said, 'Lord, give me strength for the fight'." Ward, *Sayings of the Desert Fathers*, John the Dwarf, 14, p. 75. See also Isaac, Priest of the Cells, 10, p. 86, and Joseph of Thebes, 1, p. 94.

— 24 —

Same-Sex Attraction and Sacraments

MANY CHRISTIANS WITH SAME-SEX ATTRACTIONS were baptized as children. Others were converted to Christian faith as adults. Those who become members of the Orthodox Church through adult conversion often do so because they are determined not to act on their sexual feelings and passions in ways that they understand to be opposed to divine love. In this regard they are, once again, no different from their heterosexual brothers and sisters in Christ.

Those who accept their death and resurrection with Christ in baptism, and strive to preserve "the gift of the Holy Spirit" with which they were "sealed" in chrismation, participate regularly in the Holy Eucharist. They follow the Church's liturgical cycles, attending the services, observing the Lord's Day, keeping the fasts and celebrating the feasts with obedience, gratitude, and joy. They do so in order to have the living experience of God's kingdom. Without this experience they cannot resist and abandon the pleasures and glories of the fallen world, for they will have no reason, motivation, or power to do so. "Oh, taste and see that the LORD is good!" (Ps. 34:8).[1] Without tasting the Lord's goodness, in one way or another, no person can come to know God's kingdom and overcome the fallen world.

The condition for participation in Holy Communion in the Orthodox Church is the affirmation of one's baptism and chrismation, and the unwavering determination to be faithful to these mysteries in everyday life. It is not necessary for believers to be

105

wholly successful in spiritual warfare to participate in the sacraments. For, as we have just said, virtually no one is completely successful in overcoming sinful passions in their earthly lives. But it is necessary that believers are fighting "the good fight" with the firm resolve to "finish the race" in order to receive "the crown of righteousness" that the Lord awards "to all who have loved His appearing" (2 Tim. 4:7–8).[2] Those who have given up the fight, or even worse, who do not believe that there is even a war to be fought, may not participate in Holy Communion.

In Orthodoxy, communicants in the sacramental mysteries are not only obliged to be steadfast in Christian faith and perpetually repentant over their failures, they are also obliged to take full responsibility for the Church's teachings and practices, and to be ready, at least in intention, to defend them unto death. For this reason, those who publicly affirm and promote homosexual behavior (like those who publicly advocate abortion) cannot be sacramental communicants in the Orthodox Church.[3]

A number of people with same-sex attractions, whether baptized Orthodox in childhood or converted to Orthodoxy as adults, do not "persevere to the end" in the Orthodox Church. They lose faith and fall away from the Church for many reasons, high among which may be the loss of eschatological convictions and ascetic struggles among the Church's members, especially its clergy and lay leaders. Sometimes people with same-sex desires and passions leave Orthodoxy and join churches that affirm homosexual actions as compatible with Christian faith and love. They may do this because they see no real differences between Orthodox Christians and members of other churches in their everyday lives. (The only difference they may see is some Orthodox people's attachment to their liturgical rituals and cultural traditions, their disrespect and contempt of others, and their hypocrisy about their beliefs and behaviors, including their sexual desires and activities.)

Apostolic Scriptures clearly maintain the hope that a person's exclusion from the Church's sacramental communion, whatever its reasons and ways of occurring, may ultimately serve that the person's "spirit may be saved in the day of the Lord Jesus" (1 Cor. 5:5). This is so whether a person leaves the Church's sacramental fellowship voluntarily or is excluded from participation in the sacraments by church leaders for refusing to accept the Church's understanding of Christian faith and life. When church leaders rightly remove persons from sacramental communion, they must understand their action as therapeutic and not punitive. They must be convinced that their pastoral procedure is a necessary expression of love for everyone's good, first of all the person who is asked to refrain from the sacraments.[4]

Rightly believing Christians, according to Orthodoxy, live in hope that God will save everyone as He can and that God has already done so in Christ. They know that they can "judge" only those within the Church, not those outside (see 1 Cor. 5:12–13). And they always resist the temptation to think that they know what God's final judgment will be for any person, even while professing to know the criteria of divine judgment, which they apply first of all to themselves. They also stand firm in their conviction that it is never too late for anyone to repent. And they firmly believe that no one will end up in hell unjustly or by mistake.

In a word, truly believing Christians confess that God alone judges at the end through His Son Jesus "because He is the Son of man," and that Christ's "judgment is righteous, because [He does] not seek [His] own will but the will of the Father who sent [Him]" (John 5:27–30).[5] Until God's judgment comes at the Lord's coming, the Church maintains its sacramental communion through the voluntary "unity of faith" and "communion of the Holy Spirit" among its members who are of one mind, heart, and mouth.[6]

Never forgetting that we will know only at the end who really is of God and who is not, Orthodox Christians, before all others, must remember the Lord's words that "everyone to whom much is given, from him much will be required" (Luke 12:48), and the apostolic warning that "the time has come for judgment to begin at the house of God" (1 Pet. 4:17).[7] After washing His Apostles' feet at the Last Supper, including the feet of Judas Iscariot, Jesus says to us all, "If you know these things, blessed are you if you do them" (John 13:17). We Orthodox Christians are ever ready to proclaim that we indeed "know these things." The question always remains before us, however, whether we are equally ready to answer for how we "do them." The Day will come when we will have to produce that answer.[8]

1 Also Heb. 6:4–6; 1 Pet. 2:3. The saints say that without an experience of the eternal pleasures and glories of God, no one will give up the passing pleasures and glories of this world. See St. John Climakos, *The Ladder of Divine Ascent*, 22.29, p. 135. Also, in the West, St. John of the Cross, "when a soul tastes of the spirit, it conceives a distaste for the flesh." *Living Flame of Love*, III, 39 (Garden City, NY: Doubleday Image Books, 1962), p. 231.

2 The epistle reading at several services of the Orthodox celebration of Epiphany. St. John Chrysostom asks why men dare to wear crowns, the "symbol of victory," at rites of marriage when they have already "been subdued" by *"porneia."* *On First Timothy*, Homily 9. See also Chrysostom, *On Second Timothy*, Homily 9.

3 See T. Hopko, "Eucharistic Discipline in the Orthodox Church," in *Speaking the Truth in Love*, pp. 115–117.

4 In saying this, we are aware how easily and often parents harm their children, and leaders their people, with the sick, delusional defense that they are only acting "for their own good." See Alice Miller, *For Your Own Good: Hidden Cruelty in Child-Rearing and the Roots of Violence* (New York: Farrar, Strauss and Giroux, 1990). (Orthodox Christians cannot fail to note that two of Dr. Miller's most monstrous examples of men who did massive harm to people "for their own good," including millions of murders, were baptized as infants in the Orthodox Church. Nikolai Ceaucescu was the son of an alcoholic priest who committed suicide. In his youth Joseph Stalin was an Orthodox seminarian.) This tragic travesty, however, does not alter the fact that painful actions which may appear to be punitive and harmful may in fact be expressions of "tough love" without which there can be no healing. The need for discernment is crucial.

5 From the Gospel reading at the Orthodox funeral service, John 5:24–30.

6 The Orthodox Church has no "magisterium" whose word is final. The clergy lead the Church by God's grace and power, but their leadership is not mechanical, magical, or infallible. Though the clergy normally "judge" the behavior of the faithful, especially

in regard to participation in the Church's sacraments, the clergy have sometimes themselves been proven wrong in their judgments. Thus, for example, St. Maximus the Confessor refused to participate in Holy Communion because he was convinced that the leaders of his church were in formal error concerning the Gospel. He was mutilated and tortured for his convictions, but was vindicated after his death. His teachings about Jesus became official doctrine of the Orthodox Church at the Sixth Ecumenical Council. Expressions about the "unity of the faith" and the "communion of the Holy Spirit," with the *pleroma* of the eucharistic participants being of "one mind" and "one heart" and "one mouth," are from the Divine Liturgies of St. John Chrysostom and St. Basil the Great used in the Orthodox Church.

7 In the last line of the Eucharistic Anaphora of St. Basil's Liturgy, Orthodox Christians proclaim as "God's household" that the Lord has given them all things: "Receive us all into Your kingdom, showing us to be sons of the light and sons of the day. Grant us Your peace and Your love, O Lord our God, *for You have given all things unto us.*" This, then, is also their declaration that they are ready to answer for the "all things" that they have received.

8 Every Orthodox liturgical service contains the petition to God to give those who pray "a good answer at the dread judgment seat of Christ."

— 25 —

Same-Sex Attraction and Pastoral Care

IN ORDER FOR ORTHODOX CHRISTIANS with same-sex attractions and desires to be victorious in the "unseen warfare" in which they are engaged, they have to reveal their sexual feelings to their pastors, confessors, spiritual elders, and compassionate friends. It is crucial, therefore, that the Church's priests and pastoral ministers be honest, loving, co-suffering Christians who are struggling with their own sins, confessing their own transgressions, repenting over their own failures, and receiving counsel in their own spiritual lives from their own pastors and guides. They have to be real fathers and mothers, true brothers and sisters, and genuine friends and companions to those with whom they are "work[ing] out [their] own salvation with fear and trembling" because God "works in [them] both to will and to do for His good pleasure" (Phil. 2:12–13).

It is a traditional Orthodox teaching that the Church's bishops should be men of sound doctrine and life who are extremely careful whom they ordain and appoint to priestly and pastoral service.[1] It is also a traditional Orthodox teaching that people should be extremely careful in their selection of teachers, pastors, confessors, and counselors for themselves and their children. They should never open themselves to those whom they do not trust and of whose love they are uncertain, nor should they permit their children to do so.[2] They certainly should not "come out" about their spiritual struggles, especially those of a sexual nature, with anyone of this kind. But

111

they have to "come out" to someone if they are to be supported, guided, and healed of their sinful passions and actions.[3]

Pastoral care in Orthodoxy is, by definition, the exercise of pastoral *oikonomia*.* Since no one keeps every aspect of the Christian faith perfectly and strictly, provisions have to be available, and accommodations always made, for those who are not wholly successful in their struggles. This means that pastoral *oikonomia* is for every member of the Church, in one way or another, at one time or another, without exception.[4] It also means that pastors and counselors must exercise discrimination and discernment (*diakrisis*) about what can be expected from people, given the realities of their lives. They must have the grace and the skill to know how to give counsel that realistically assists people in their spiritual enlightenment and growth.[5] It also means that they will at times have to practice patience and endurance with sinful behavior, while never sanctioning it, as people struggle to sort things out, see things clearly, admit the realities of their lives, and commit themselves completely to growing up to "the measure of the stature of the fullness of Christ" (Eph. 4:13).

For persons with same-sex attractions in our time, given all that is now occurring in our gravely disordered world, Orthodox Christian pastoral care requires extraordinary discernment, patience, compassion, and love. It calls for an extraordinary capacity to listen and hear, to see and understand, to say true things with love, and to suffer patiently, often in painful, prayerful, hopeful silence. It demands a willingness on the part of pastors, parents, counselors, and friends not simply to "go the extra mile" with their friends and relatives with same-sex attractions, but to carry on with them until the end, no matter what. Such pastoral care requires being constantly tested concerning one's own faith and love, one's refusal to condemn others, and one's readiness to give one's life so that others

---

* Unfortunately, there is no appropriate English equivalent for *oikonomia*. See note 5 for an explanation.

may live. It also requires that Christians with same-sex attractions exercise love and patience with their counselors, listening to them attentively, and praying fervently that they will serve them well and bring no harm upon them.

Because the majority of those who consider themselves Christians today, including the majority of members of Orthodox churches, have hardly been evangelized and instructed in the Christian faith, proper pastoral care with wise discernment (*diakrisis*) and appropriate *oikonomia* are extremely hard to come by. And because our time is also so dominated by people whose sole criteria of behavior are their subjective feelings and experiences informed by what they take to be the latest results of modern science, spiritual care and friendship, even from one's parents and pastors, are extraordinarily difficult to find and fulfill.

Orthodoxy holds, however, that those desiring guidance and support in the way of Christ and the Holy Spirit will find and receive it. The sayings, "When the disciple is ready, the master appears," and "The elder's mouth is opened by the seeker's insistence," are Orthodox Christian convictions, based on the Lord's promises, that have proven true in the lives of countless people. And, as the holy elders themselves unanimously testify, we all have the Scriptures, the church services, and the writings and examples of the saints by which God's Logos/Son and Spirit can guide us when wise elders are absent. The condition for our being led, of course, is that we are truly humble and authentically willing to be taught, directed, and healed by God.[6]

---

1 "Tell me, where do you think all the disorders of the church originate? I think their only origin is in the careless and random way in which the prelates [bishops and priests] are chosen and appointed." St. John Chrysostom, *On the Priesthood*, Book 3.10; see also Book 4.1–2 (Crestwood, NY: SVS Press, 1984), pp. 79, 104–113. Orthodox canons follow the qualifications for ordination found in 1 Tim. 3:1–13 and Titus 1:5–9. In regard to sexual requirements, the Orthodox rule is that only once-married men and celibates may be bishops and priests. Since the sixth century, bishops have to be

unmarried. Celibate candidates for ordination have to be virgins, and married men (and their spouses) have to have been virgins at the time of their marriage. Today, for obvious reasons, *oikonomia* is often practiced in regard to the canons requiring virginity. Men with same-sex attractions may be ordained if their feelings are under control and are not being acted upon. The same is true for men who have troubles with sexual purity in regard to women. It may also be noted that men and women with same-sex attractions may be married to persons of the opposite sex if their same-sex feelings are disciplined and their spouses are willing to support them in their sexual life, as well as in their struggles with other feelings that accompany sexual difficulties, such as shame, guilt, anger, sadness, despondency, disappointment, and self-interest.

2 See St. John Climakos, *The Ladder of Divine Ascent*, 4:6, 120.

3 I am not saying here that people may, or at times even *should*, hide their sins from their confessors. I am saying that they should never go to confession to a priest they do not trust. It is possible, however, in rare situations, that a sort of reversal of pastoral *oikonomia* may be in order, in which a penitent would not hide anything from his confessor, but still would not go deeply into his sins, especially sins of a sexual nature (which the holy fathers unanimously teach should, in any case, never be spoken of in detail), with a priest whom he discerns, for any number of reasons, to be unable to handle his confession. In such rare cases it is imperative that such a penitent quickly find a priest/confessor with whom he or she can be completely open (without violating the counsel to refrain from describing specific details of sexual sins).

4 *Oikonomia* is not a dispensation from God's laws or an abrogation of God's commandments. On the contrary, *oikonomia* is precisely the proper application of God's laws and commandments to persons in situations where, for any number of reasons, the commandments and laws cannot be strictly followed. The purpose of *oikonomia* is the salvation of people's lives. It is applied by wise pastors with discrimination and discernment in order to assist, enable, and empower people to make the next step on their uniquely personal path of spiritual (and psychological, emotional, physical, and sexual) growth and maturation in divine life and love.

5 In English translations of Orthodox spiritual literature, *diakrisis* is translated as both "discrimination" and "discernment." The saints consider this gift to be the most important of virtues. It results from long labors in attaining and securing God's grace. It is the product of humility and "a broken and contrite heart." Indeed, according to the saints, no one can have *diakrisis* without a "wounded" or "painful" or "broken" heart. Many may have ascetic achievements, the saints teach, but few have *diakrisis*. People may be appointed to teach from books without discernment, St. John Climakos contends, but no one without it should exercise pastoral authority or engage in pastoral and spiritual counseling. St. John Climakos, *The Ladder of Divine Ascent*, Step 26. See also Anthony the Great, 8, and Syncletica, 17, in *The Sayings of the Desert Fathers*. Also John Cassian, *On the Holy Fathers of Sketis and "On Discrimination" written for Abba Leontius*; and Peter of Damascus, "True Discrimination" in *A Treasury of Divine Knowledge* and "Discrimination" in *Twenty-four Discourses*, all of which may be found in the British

translation of the *Philokalia* (London: Faber and Faber, 1979, 1984). See also Saints Barsanuphios and John, *Guidance Toward Spiritual Life* (Platina: St. Herman of Alaska Brotherhood, 1990), pp. 262–264.

6 Ps. 25:9. See, once again, St. Ignatius Brianchaninoff, *The Arena,* throughout.

— 26 —

Same-Sex Attraction and the Counseling Process

WHEN ASKED ABOUT PRACTICAL ELEMENTS in pastoral care for Christians with same-sex attractions, whether or not they are acting on them, I would offer the following convictions, which I believe are in full accord with traditional Orthodox teaching and practice.

Those exercising Christian pastoral care must love the people who come to them with this issue. They must identify with them. They must respect them. They must listen to them. They must put themselves in their place. They must feel the other's pain and suffering more than they do their own. They must advocate for them before God. They must be ready, if called, even to give their life for them. Pastoral counselors must also be aware of the enormous pressure on these people to affirm and act on their feelings, even to see the feelings as blessed expressions of God's essential goodwill toward them and others with the same desires. The counselors must be as aware as possible of the arguments, often brilliant and compelling, employed to defend the propriety and godliness of same-sex attraction and erotic activity, including the way the Bible is interpreted to defend such desires and affirm their enactment.

Orthodox Christian counselors must also realize how painful and difficult it is for persons with same-sex attractions, despite the forcefulness and bravado they may display, to speak about their feelings and actions with a "church person." And perhaps most important of all, the pastoral counselor must demonstrate from the very beginning that persons who come for assistance and guidance are

totally free in their coming, and, as we said, totally loved and re-
spected. Counselors must make them know and feel that they are
under no pressure of any kind to be there, even when they may in
fact be compelled to the counseling by parents, spouses, family
members, or anyone else. And the counselor must ensure confi-
dence in the complete confidentiality of what occurs in their meet-
ings together.

Christian counselors must abandon all stereotyping of people
with same-sex attractions. They must see each person as the unique
person he or she is, each with his or her own unique inheritance
and history. They must recognize the indescribable complexity of
the issue of sexuality generally, and same-sex attraction in particular, however certain some speakers and writers may be in their opinions on the subject. They must resist every temptation to oversim-
plify. They must dread being overly confident in their evaluations.
They must discard all anecdotal materials and all textbook theories
on the subject, while being as much aware of all of them as they can.

Christian counselors must never view same-sex attraction and
sexual activity as any more or less shocking or abhorrent than other
feelings and actions that Orthodox Christianity considers sinful.
They must surely distinguish radically between a person's feelings
and actions, between what one feels and does willfully and voluntarily, and what one does by passionate compulsion. And they must
never forget that God alone knows the culpability of every person's
thoughts, words, feelings, and actions.

Christian counselors always begin with prayerful questioning
and listening. They never begin by preaching, teaching, prophesying, or pronouncing judgments. They start by learning as much
about the person and his or her family as they can. They take all the
time they need to do this, using all the skills available to them. They
are in no hurry. They ask and listen, and listen and ask some
more. They try to hear the person's spoken words, to read his or her
body language, and to heed his or her silences. They do not force

admissions or disclosures of any kind. And, of course, they should themselves be free of all prurient interests. Their first goal, without which nothing fruitful can occur, is to build up a communion of trust and mutual understanding that would enable the person to speak freely, without fear of reprisal in any form. They should never engage in debating and quarrelling.

Before any discussion of specifically sexual issues, both theoretical and actual, and after learning as much as possible about the person and his or her story, the first conversations between the counselor and the person who comes for counseling must be about Christ and the Gospel. The counselor must find out what the person knows, thinks, and believes about the Christian faith. The counselor must learn the person's spiritual history and become aware of the person's theological ideas. The counselor must also come to know what the person knows and thinks about the Bible, and about the sacraments, services, and saints of the Church. A crucial goal early in the process is to have the person come to see that he or she and the counselor are not in a debate over who is right and who is wrong, but are rather engaged in a conversation about *what* is right and *what* is wrong for them together, and for everyone else as well.

The counselor and the one counseled must be convinced that their meeting is not about enforcing the teachings and rules of the Church, and still less those of the Church's leaders. Their encounter is rather about what God wills for His people as revealed in Jesus Christ and the Holy Spirit. They are in communion as friends, co-sinners and co-strugglers who are seeking the same thing, namely God's will for them in the actual conditions of their actual lives.

It must also be clearly evident that Orthodox counselors are fully ready to admit that they may be wrong in their convictions, in their evaluations, and in their counsel and advice. Of course, the counselors should be convinced of what they think, say, and do, and never say or do anything of which they are not sure and for which they are not prepared to take full responsibility before God, and before the person and his or her family. But, in the end, Orthodox Christian counselors can only stand on their convictions with full responsibility, and let those who come to them decide for themselves what they will do, or not do, about them.[1]

Regarding the counseling process itself, the first concrete goal of counseling with people having same-sex attractions, just as with anyone else, is to persuade the counselee to stop his or her sinful behavior. It is crucial, before anything else, that the person being counseled ceases "acting out." Often, if not always, the agreement to stop the behavior, or at least to try to stop, will be undertaken on faith rather than conviction. The person will agree to do so because he or she trusts the advice of the counselor as he or she comes to believe that, according to the Christian faith, the cessation of a sinful action is a necessary condition for understanding its sinfulness.

The point here is simple and evident. While any one of us is engaging in destructive behavior, we are incapable of seeing and thinking clearly and fruitfully, and, as such, we are incapable of understanding the nature of our wrongdoing and the causes for its presence and power in our lives. We remain blinded and bound by our actions, which preclude any constructive conversations about them. To talk with an alcoholic who is actively drinking, for example, or with an overeater who is overeating, or a fornicator who is fornicating, is a waste of time and energy that cannot possibly bring fruitful results. The first talking, therefore, and the first goal of counseling, always has to do with actions, not attitudes. It is about behavior, not beliefs.

Although pastoral counseling is not the time for preaching, teaching, prophesying, or making judgments, and surely never begins with these things, instruction and exhortation are always a necessary part of the process. The counselor addresses the mind of the person, and also the heart and will. This may take considerable time, even many years. But the time has to be taken if the process is to be effective and fruitful. For when disagreements or misunderstandings about the content of the Christian faith exist and persist, what possible purpose could be served in talking about sex? And, as we have also just said, when people are acting sinfully, what use can be served by talking theoretically about sin?

Counseling sessions with persons having same-sex attractions, as with all persons, should be disciplined in regard to time, content, and interaction. They should be regular. They should be cordial and friendly, but rigorous in observing personal freedoms and personal boundaries. They should be conducted in an atmosphere of mutual love and trust. And I personally agree with those who insist that the parties in the counseling process should be of the same sex.

During the counseling process, the person should be kept as fully within the sacramental life of the Church as possible. It may be necessary, however, as we indicated above, for the person to abstain from participation in the Eucharist when his or her convictions and actions are in conscious and willful contradiction to the Church's doctrine and discipline. If there is any question about this, the benefit of the doubt belongs to the person being counseled. And, of course, if the person persists in sinful actions, but repents of them sincerely, he or she must be continually welcomed into Holy Communion with complete assurance of the Lord's forgiveness and mercy.

It may happen, in the end, that the person concludes that he or she does not believe in the Christian faith as taught and practiced in the Orthodox Church. In such instances, as we have already stated, the counselor must assure the person that he or she is not judged or condemned in any way, and that he or she is welcome to come to church services and to continue in friendly relations. Counselees must also be assured that they may continue in ongoing dialogue, if they so desire. The only reason to break relations with the person, and even to exclude him or her from church gatherings, is if he or she is openly propagating teachings and practices contrary to Orthodoxy and, as such, may do harm to others in the community, especially younger people. In such cases, there is no difference in the Church's discipline in regard to a person with same-sex attractions and actions from anyone else engaging in teachings and deeds that Orthodoxy considers to be contrary to God and dangerous to people.

1 A striking example of this attitude is found in the Life of St. Maximos the Confessor. When the saint was asked to condemn his adversaries—including emperors and bishops, with whom he refused to participate in Holy Communion, and to pronounce them as being wicked people—he refused to do so. He said that God would judge them. The only thing he knew, he insisted, was that he could not agree with them or commune with them because he was convinced that they were betraying the Gospel and the conciliar teachings that were universally accepted by the Orthodox Church.

— 27 —

Same-Sex Attraction and Christian Witness Today

ALL HUMAN BEINGS, including those with same-sex feelings and desires, have to decide in which human community they belong and to which human community they give their heart. If they are Christians, they have to decide which church is most faithful to the true God and the real Jesus. They have to decide where the Holy Spirit acts with power. They have to decide who are their pastors, teachers, and friends, their sisters and brothers in Christ. They have to decide who are the saints they will honor, obey, and strive to emulate. They have to decide where the life is that they want to live, the abundant life (John 10:10) that Christ gives, the "life which is life indeed" (1 Tim. 6:19, RSV). This means they have to decide where divine love is, what it is, how it is, who it is, and what it demands of people who believe in the God who is Love.

The witness of Orthodox Christianity in the present world demands that there be Orthodox Christian men and women struggling by God's grace to resist expressing their love for people of their own sex in sexual actions that some claim to be loving, but that they believe are betrayals of divine love. Humanity needs this courageous testimony more than ever before in its history. Those whom God calls to this ascetic feat are chosen to fight on the front lines of the spiritual battle of our time. They are among those most obviously called to be martyrs and confessors for Christ in humanity's present condition. They, perhaps more than all others today, are blessed to bear witness to the truth that humanity's enemy is everywhere and always the same for everyone.

Humanity's enemy is the self-love, self-will, self-affirmation, and self-delusion that dominate human being and life in this corrupted and disordered world, which lies in the power of evil.[1] The enemy is "the wisdom of this world" (*sophia tou cosmou*) and "the wisdom of men" (*sophia anthropon*), which lead to sin and death (1 Cor. 1:20; 2:5). It is the earthly, psychic, and diabolical wisdom (*he sophia . . . epigeios, psychiki, daimoniodes*) that is opposed to God's wisdom, which "is from above" (*anothen katerchomeni*, James 3:15–17). It is, ultimately, the "human gospel," the "gospel according to man" (*to evangelion kata anthropon*) of those who worship "the god of this age" (*ho theos tou aionos toutou*) that they themselves have made, or that others have inflicted upon them in place of the true and living God who made them (Gal. 1:11; 2 Cor. 4:4).

Humanity's enemy, finally, using the biblical word, is the devil. It is the "murderer from the beginning," the "father of lies" who "does not stand in the truth, because there is no truth in him" (John 8:44). It is the "wicked one" in whose power the "whole world lies" (1 John 5:19), from whom Christians pray to be delivered in the prayer given to them by their Lord (Matt. 6:13).[2] It is "Satan, and all his works, and all his angels, and all his service, and all his pride," which Christians renounce and spit upon at their baptisms.[3] It is the one that Christ came to crush on the cross: "For this purpose the Son of God was manifested, that He might destroy the works of the devil" (1 John 3:8).

Orthodox Christians believe every human being is called to conquer humanity's enemy through God's power. They believe this is possible through Christ, who is Himself "the power of God" that conquers (1 Cor. 1:24).[4] Christians consciously avail themselves of God's power in Christ by being crucified to the world with Jesus and by being raised with Him to "newness of life" (Gal. 6:14; Rom. 6:3–4). They are convinced that this is all God wants of them and for them. Their only prayer, therefore, is Christ's own: "Abba, Father, all things are possible for You. Take this cup away from Me; nevertheless, not what I will, but what You will" (Mark 14:36).

Orthodox Christians "long for the resurrection of the dead and the life of the age to come" (Nicene Creed). They expect to rejoice forever with all who have followed God's Word, however they have come to know it and do it. They are convinced that all who are saved, however God provides for that wonder to be, will know that they have been saved by the broken body and spilled blood of Jesus.[5] Whoever they are, they will be those who have known how "wretched, miserable, poor, blind, and naked" they were on this earth, and how desperately in need they were of salvation and healing. They will be people from all tribes and nations "who come out of the great tribulation" and "washed their robes and made them white in the blood of the Lamb," perhaps not even knowing this is what they were doing when they fought their sinful passions and endured their afflictions on earth for the sake of love, truth, and righteousness (Rev. 3:17; 7:11–14). They will enter the Lamb's bridal chamber and partake of His marriage supper as "virgins" (Rev. 14:1–5). They will be the Lamb's "wife" in the unending age when "marrying and being given in marriage" will be no more.

In the new heaven and new earth of God's new creation in Christ, who makes all things new, all who love Divine Love will be one with Him in a communion of love in the Holy Spirit that grows fuller, deeper, and ever more glorious for all eternity.[6]

The Spirit and the bride say, "Come!"
And let him who hears say, "Come!" (Rev. 22:17)

Amen. Even so, come, Lord Jesus! (Rev. 22:20)

And we know that the Son of God has come and has given us an understanding, that we may know Him who is true;

and we are in Him who is true, in His Son Jesus Christ. This is the true God and eternal life. Little children, keep yourselves from idols. Amen. (1 John 5:20–21)

1 "Self-love" (*philautia*) is not the positive and proper godly love of self that human beings must have as God's good creatures for whom Christ has died. *Philautia* is rather the sinful self-love that is contrary to the love of God and neighbor. St. Maximus the Confessor taught that *philautia* is humanity's primordial sin, and the cause of all sins and miseries. See, for example, St. Maximus the Confessor, *Third Century on Love*, 7–11, 56–57. See also L. Thunberg, *Microcosm and Mediato: The Theological Anthropology of Maximus the Confessor* (Lund: C.W.K. Gleerup, 1965), pp. 244–262.

2 Matt. 6:13. Most church fathers and contemporary scholars think that the "*apo tou ponirou*" at the end of the prayer is not to be translated into English as generic "evil," but as "the evil one." See Thomas Hopko, *The Lord's Prayer* [Audio recordings on CD] (Crestwood, NY, SVS Press, 2004).

3 The renunciation in the rite of exorcism at Orthodox baptism (New York: Department of Religious Education, Orthodox Church in America, 1972, 1983), p. 39.

4 The word for *save* and *conquer* is the same word in Hebrew. Conquering, triumphing, and being victorious are synonymous in Scripture with being saved. See the letters to the churches and the images of the Lamb's war in the Apocalypse. See also Rom. 8:37 and 1 John 5:4–5.

5 The Great Prokeimenon at Vespers on the evening of every Great Feast of the Orthodox Church—Pascha, Pentecost, Christmas, and Theophany—is the psalm verse, "Who is so great a God as our God; You are the God who works wonders" (Psalm 77:14). The entire psalm powerfully proclaims that the greatest and most marvelous wonder the Lord has performed is the salvation of His weary, moaning, uncomforted, fainting, troubled, grieving, and apparently forgotten, spurned, and abandoned people.

6 Rev. 3:17; 14:1–5; 19—22 and throughout. On the teaching of unending growth and perfection in divine glory, see the mystical writings of St. Gregory of Nyssa, especially his commentaries *On the Beatitudes, On the Song of Songs,* and *On the Life of Moses.* Selections from these writings may be found in English in *From Glory to Glory: Texts from Gregory of Nyssa's Mystical Writings*, selected and with an introduction by Jean Danielou, translated and edited by Herbert Musurillo (New York: Scribners, 1961).